WHAT A YEAR IT WAS!

1960

A walk back in time to revisit
what life was like in the year that
has special meaning for you...

*Congratulations
and
Best Wishes*

9/17/60

To Barbara & Jesse Newson

From Bill & Marlene Lacy

DEDICATION

To My Son, Lee:
The joy, talent, love, humor and gift of wisdom you bring to the world
is incalculable. Thanks for being the son every mother hopes for.
Happy 40th Birthday
Love,
Mom

A SPECIAL REMEMBRANCE FOR JOHN F. KENNEDY, JR. —
Born four days before my son, he would have turned 40 this year.
I always had a very special place in my heart for John and
watched him develop into a superior human being.
His untimely passing touched me deeply.

Designers • **Peter Hess & Marguerite Jones**

Research and Special Segments Writer • **Laurie Cohn**

CONTENTS

President Eisenhower's STATE OF THE UNION ADDRESS

Congress warmly welcomes President Eisenhower.

Mrs. Eisenhower *(right)* and Mrs. Nixon are among the spectators.

President Eisenhower gives his annual State Of The Union message predicting a boom in the economy, revealing spectacular advances in development of the Atlas missile and reviewing the prospects for peace.

1960

The American Nazi Party

Denied Right To Hold A Rally On July 4th By New York Mayor Robert F. Wagner.

- **CITING REFUSAL TO USE FEDERAL FUNDS,** President Eisenhower vetoes bill to reverse river pollution.

- **THE 23RD AMENDMENT** banning poll tax receives Senate approval.

- **IKE REQUESTS $4.1 BILLION** for foreign aid.

CIVIL RIGHTS

SEGREGATION / INTEGRATION / BUSSING / PROTESTS / SIT-INS / COURTS

In A Vote Of 288 To 95 The U.S. House Of Representatives Passes A Compromise Civil Rights Act.

After A Long Battle, The U.S. Congress Sends Civil Rights Bill To White House.

President Eisenhower Signs The Civil Rights Act Of 1960.

Integration Of Dallas Schools Ordered By U.S. District Judge T.W. Davidson To Commence In September 1961.

Despite Strong Southern Protests, The Democratic Party Includes A Strong Civil Rights Plank.

Delay In Integrating Schools In Houston And New Orleans Denied By U.S. Supreme Court.

Louisiana State Senate Passes Laws To Block School Integration In New Orleans. Federal Court Issues Restraining Order.

Four Negro* Girls Are Escorted Into Two Desegregated White Schools In New Orleans By Federal Marshals.

In An Historic Appointment, NAACP Chairman Robert Weaver Is Appointed Administrator Of The Housing And Home Finance Agency Becoming The Highest-Ranking Negro To Hold A Federal Administrative Post.

The Supreme Court Rules That It Is A Violation Of The Interstate Commerce Act For Bus Terminal Restaurants To Refuse To Serve Negroes.

Measures Taken To Block Desegregation Of Louisiana Schools Ruled Illegal By U.S. Supreme Court.

* Negro was the commonly used term in 1960.

WHAT A YEAR IT WAS!

Why is this famous Paris rendezvous called "the American Bar"?

A favorite meeting place of Americans in Paris is the bar of the Hotel Ritz. It is called, in fact, "the American Bar." And it lives up to its name by serving the traditional American drink...fine Bourbon whiskey. As the picture shows, smart Europeans like it, too.

Here in the U.S.A. the trend to Bourbon is unmistakable. People have discovered that Bourbon has more taste because it is *all* whiskey and *all* aged. It is the only whiskey so smooth that it is at its best bottled right from the cask.

People who know whiskey and know their own minds prefer Bourbon. They will tell you it has more flavor. And now that it is available in the popular moderate proofs, *millions* of people have switched from other whiskies to Bourbon. But have you ever heard of a Bourbon drinker changing to anything else?

While the American Bar has traveled abroad, it is still an institution in the U.S.A.—a center of sociability from coast to coast. And whatever your favorite Bourbon drink, you'll find it served at its best in your favorite tavern.

THE BOURBON INSTITUTE
dedicated to bringing world-wide recognition to a great American tradition

7

Well-Travelled Nikita Khrushchev Visits *Paris*

Mr. K. and his entourage arrive at Orly Airport for an 11-day state visit and are met by President de Gaulle.

The first Russian government chief in France since Czar Nicholas in 1896, Mr. K's visit indicates acceptance of France as a full-fledged great power, a personal victory for President de Gaulle, and will include pre-summit talks between the two leaders radically different in personality and philosophy.

Parisians line the street to catch a glimpse of the Russian ruler whose public speeches contain flattering words about France as well as warnings against German militarism.

Security precautions, as heavy as any in recent history, are in effect weeks before Khrushchev's arrival.

An essential part of Khrushchev's itinerary is a visit to the Arc de Triomphe where he pays tribute to the grave of the Unknown Soldier of France.

A stirring memorial and reminder to the men who sway their nation's destinies of the grief and horrors of past wars.

Spying Over Russia

Secret reconnaissance of Russia by high-flying American U-2 jet ends when one is downed deep in Soviet territory putting East-West relations into a diplomatic tailspin. At first the U.S. denies spying calling it a weather plane. The U.S. recants and admits the U-2 flight was a spying mission.

Powers' conviction is inevitable and he is sentenced to 10 years in prison. The U-2 affair becomes Khrushchev's pretext to torpedo the Big 4 Paris Summit conference and bars President Eisenhower from Russia.

With his family in the courtroom U-2 pilot Gary Francis Powers is charged with espionage against the Soviet Union and is the subject of a showcase trial.

Mr. K's ultimatums to the Big Three representatives — *(left to right)* President de Gaulle, Prime Minister Macmillan and President Eisenhower — overplays his propaganda advantage.

☭ Leonid I. Brezhnev succeeds Marshal Voroshilov as titular Chief of State of the U.S.S.R.

☭ Soviet Premier Nikita Khrushchev is greeted with cheers and confetti as 100,000 Afghans line up to glimpse the Russian leader in his motorcade.

☭ Ten nations meet in Geneva to discuss disarmament — Soviet Bloc lukewarm to Western proposals.

☭ Khrushchev names 54-year old Leonid I. Brezhnev Chairman of the Presidium after Alexei N. Kosygin becomes first Deputy Premier in the Soviet Government.

Nikita Khrushchev

☭ Nikita Khrushchev announces that his country has nuclear submarines with capabilities of launching nuclear weapons.

Leningrad

Moscow

Kiev

U.S.S.R.

Nikita Khrushchev continues his boisterous boorish tactics *(above)* targeting Britain's Prime Minister Macmillan *(right)*.

Mr. K along with other Soviet representatives bang on their tables in protest over the proceedings. At a session of the U.N. General Assembly in an angry gesture he pounds his shoe on the table.

Dag Hammarskjold wins free men's admiration with his defiance of Russian attacks on his handling of the Congo crisis.

UNITED

U.N. GENERAL ASSEMBLY GOES INTO SESSION WITH MANY HEADS OF STATE IN ATTENDANCE.

NIKITA KHRUSHCHEV DEMANDS THE UNITED NATIONS BE REMOVED FROM THE UNITED STATES AND A NEW SECRETARY GENERAL REPLACE DAG HAMMARSKJOLD.

WHAT A YEAR IT WAS!

1960

Among the world leaders attending the General Assembly session are Egypt's Abdul Nasser *(left)* and Yugoslavia's Marshal Tito. All are vying for the friendship and support of 15 newly admitted African states.

One of the most fateful of many informal meetings in New York was between Khrushchev and Cuba's Fidel Castro.

NATIONS

The Russian/Cuban threat to the Western Hemisphere solidarity is background for President Eisenhower's talks with Pan-American leaders.

CASTRO ASSAILS THE UNITED STATES IN A FOUR-HOUR SPEECH BEFORE THE U.N. GENERAL ASSEMBLY.

A RESOLUTION TO END WORLD TENSIONS AND CREATE HARMONY IS PASSED BY THE U.N. GENERAL ASSEMBLY.

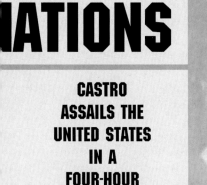

Castro is closely aligned with the Communist Party *(below left)* and seizes almost all United States property in Cuba *(below right)*.

WHAT A YEAR IT WAS!

MAY DAY IN BERLIN

In Communist East Berlin The Traditional May Day Parade Is Staged As A Five-Hour Military Operation

250,000 Germans gather to watch some 35,000 goose-stepping troops and a rumbling array of heavy armor and artillery.

Under a banner that reads "Down With German Militarism" the Red forces march in a show of military muscle barely two weeks before the summit talks are scheduled to begin.

Less than a mile away in free West Berlin, nearly a million assemble led by Mayor Willy Brandt.

In the biggest outpouring of West Berliners since the war, the slogan is "Freedom For All."

Informally staged in contrast to the East Berlin rally, this May Day demonstration is an impressive answer to Khrushchev's renewed tough talk on the German issue.

Mayor Brandt tells the nations of the free world that the people of his city are determined to remain their own masters.

75,000 Brits stage demonstration protesting nuclear weapons and call for unilateral British disarmament.

Bonn government arrests anti-Semitic rioters.

The French test their first Atomic Bomb in Southern Algeria and despite protests from the U.S. and the United Nations, de Gaulle orders the continuation of the A-Bomb program.

The day before talks are to take place between Khrushchev and de Gaulle, France explodes her second A-Bomb.

The European Free Trade Association is established by Austria, Britain, Denmark, Norway, Portugal, Sweden and Switzerland.

Poland to pay $40 million to the U.S. for illegal seizure of U.S. property.

You'll look a long time before matching Mercury's beauty at such a low price

THE BIG REASON FOR MERCURY'S POPULARITY is obvious, above. What other car even approaches its fresh, clean beauty?

But beyond this, there is a value story that seems almost unbelievable when you first read the price tag. For example, Mercury's dramatic price reductions for 1960 now place the de luxe-equipped Monterey in the same price range as "dolled-up" models of low-priced cars.

But what a lot more car the same money buys with Mercury!

Mercury moves in a smoother, quieter way than "so-called" low-priced cars. Its wheelbase is 7 inches longer for greater road stability. Exclusive 3-phase shock absorbers take the beating that you take in other cars. Up to 23% more insulation surrounds you with restful quiet.

Mercury advantages are everywhere. There's more room to stretch out in; more foot room for center-seat passengers. Interiors are more luxurious. Brakes are bigger—and self-adjusting. The largest windshield on any car means better visibility. And Mercury's super-efficient standard engine delivers far more "go"—and on regular gas.

But most important, no other car in America is better built. To safeguard quality, *every single* Mercury is road-tested before it is approved for shipment. None of Mercury's competitors takes such care. All low-priced and medium-priced cars rely on spot-checking. So stop in at Quality Headquarters, your Mercury dealer's. See all the extra values Mercury offers you for low-price-field money!

16

☆ Havana

Fidel
Castro

1960

SOUTH AMERICA

◎ **On his four-nation South American tour President Eisenhower is greeted in Santiago, Chile by an enormously enthusiastic crowd.**

◎ **Ike is greeted by pro-Castro banners in Montevideo, Uruguay.**

◎ **Brasilia replaces Rio de Janeiro as capital of Brazil.**

◎ **To reinforce Panama's titular sovereignty, President Eisenhower orders its flag flown alongside the U.S. flag in the Panama Canal.**

◎ **Guatemala and Nicaragua accuse Cuba's Castro of inciting uprisings — Ike orders U.S. Navy to Caribbean.**

✺ Official U.S. Policy Remains No Reprisals Against Cuba Or Any Intervention In Its Internal Affairs.

✺ The Soviets Sign An Agreement With Castro To Import Cuban Sugar The Importation Of Which Is Cut By 95% In America.

✺ President Eisenhower Authorizes Training Of Cuban Exiles By The CIA For The Purpose Of Toppling The Cuban Government.

✺ It Is Alleged That Chicago Mafia Leader Sam Giancana Is Approached By The CIA To Get Rid Of Castro.

✺ Cuba Holds Largest Mass Military Trial In History Convicting 104 People As Enemies Of The Government.

✺ The United States Terminates Economic Aid To Cuba.

✺ The Monroe Doctrine Is Declared Dead By The Soviets Who Throw Their Full Support Behind Cuba In Any Attempt To Eliminate The U.S. Naval Base At Guantanamo.

✺ Cuban Patrol Boat Fires On A U.S. Submarine.

✺ French Munitions Freighter Explodes In Havana Harbor Killing 75 People — Castro Denounces U.S. With Accusations Of Complicity.

✺ U.S. State Department Warns U.S. Citizens To Avoid Travelling To Cuba.

✺ Over 1,000 Cubans Flee To The U.S. Weekly Seeking Freedom.

✺ A Cuban Firing Squad Executes U.S. Citizen Anthony Zarba And Seven Cubans After Convicting Them On Charges Of Participating In The Cuban Invasion.

✺ Land Mines Are Placed Around Guantanamo By The U.S. Navy.

Frenchmen clash with Frenchmen over Algerian self-determination.

Despite the enormous conflict, the policy is being carried forward by President de Gaulle who, acting under special decree powers, takes steps to curb riots in Algeria, including dissolution of the Algerian home guard and the institution of wide reforms.

SOUTH AFRICA

Native Protests Flare Up Against Apartheid And Passbook Laws All Over South Africa.

100 people die when police fire on demonstrators in Sharpeville, a city near Johannesburg, and in the largest mass round-up in South African history 1,500 demonstrators are arrested in Nyanga, outside of Capetown.

An assassination attempt against Premier Verwoerd is made by a white farmer.

Verwoerd survives, apartheid continues and South Africa is in turmoil.

Turbulence In Africa As Former European Colonies Gain Their Independence

Independence comes to over a dozen African states peaceably, but in the Belgian Congo freedom is followed by rioting and army mutiny *(1,2)*.

Replacing Belgian forces in Katanga, United Nations troops are called in to avert total chaos *(3)*. For months the political pattern keeps changing with kaleidoscopic speed.

Pro-Red Premier Lumumba, who claims votes to form the Congo government *(4)*, is seized by the forces of Colonel Mobutu *(5)*, but the power struggle continues.

1960
The End Of EMPIRE

CAMEROO proclaims independ from France with day being marked renewed violence.

U.S. investments in **South Africa** reported at $3 million.

U.S. condemns police action against demonstrators **South Africa**.

British House Of Commons passes a resolution deplori **South Africa's** racial policies.

Anglican Bishop of Johannesburg exiled for his oppositi to apartheid.

In **South Africa** whites vote to become a republ Nelson Mandela's African National Congress party banned.

Kwame Nkrumah is president of **Ghana** as it becom a republic in the British Commonwealth.

Police in **Kenya** arrest 100 Mau-Mau aides in Nairo

France agrees to withdraw from its military bases **Morocco**.

Poet Leopold Senghor is elected first president of the ne republic of **Senegal**, former French colony in W Africa.

British Commonwealth nation of **Nigeria** gets ind pendence.

French Rule in **Algeria** is favored by 200 French intellectuals who sign manifesto.

- Joseph Kasavubu selected to form first Congolese government.
- Europeans flee as Congo army rebels oust all Belgian officers.
- Premiere Moise Tshombe declares Katanga province's independence from Congo and requests aid from Belgium.
- U.N. Chief Dag Hammarskjold arrives in the Congo.
- Congo's Lumumba excluded as Kasavubu wins seat at the U.N.
- In Brazzaville Congo Republic declares independence from France.
- Under the leadership of Colonel Mobutu, the Congolese army takes control.

Students Riot In JAPAN

Japanese fanatic students and leftist groups riot for four days in protest over the Mutual Defense Treaty with America.

Attempts to physically prevent the signing of the treaty fail as the Speaker is carried to the platform and calls to order the session that approves the treaty. Violence continues causing the cancellation of a visit by President Eisenhower after White House Secretary James C. Hagerty's car is surrounded by a mob keeping him imprisoned for 80 minutes before a U.S. helicopter rescues him.

Strongly opposed to the treaty, Socialist leader Inejiro Asanuma *(above)* is fatally stabbed by a right-wing student *(right)*.

Stormy Aftermath To Elections In

Following Syngman Rhee's landslide victory for his fourth term in office, a mob of thousands clash with police.

KOREA

The Battle For LAOS

Vientiane, capital city of Laos, lies in ruins after the battle in which government troops hurled back Communist Pathet Lao rebel troops.

The United States Embassy is among the structures gutted.

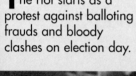

The riot starts as a protest against balloting frauds and bloody clashes on election day.

Victory in the capital city has not ended conflict in this strategic Southeast Asian country. Communist military aid is being poured in and a full-scale propaganda barrage is being waged against American assistance to the Laotian government.

With 115 dead in riots in this new political crisis and turbulence, at the urging of the United States, Syngman Rhee, one of the fathers of the Republic, finally resigns his presidency.

The situation grows more ominous daily at this focal point of conflict between Communism and the free world.

WHAT A YEAR IT WAS!

21

Mongolia

☆Ulaan Baatar

Japan

☆Tokyo

Korea

Peking☆

Seoul☆

China

Shanghai☆

Tibet

Nepal

India

☆Calcutta

Burma

Laos

Vietnam

Philippines

Manila☆

ombay

Rangoon☆

Thailand

Bangkok☆

Cambodia

Phnom Penh☆ ☆Saigon

Ceylon

Pro-West Supporter Hayato Ikeda Replaces Assassinated Nobusuke Kishi As Japanese Premier.

After Six Days Of Talks India's Prime Minister Nehru And China's Premier Chou En-lai Fail To Solve Their Border Dispute.

Communist China Found Guilty By The International Commission Of Jurists Of Attempting The Destruction Of The Buddhist Religion In Tibet.

Trying To Demonstrate Good Faith, The Chinese Negotiate A Border Treaty With Nepal.

The Chinese Conclude A Border Treaty With Burma.

Ceylon's New Prime Minister Mrs. Sirimavo Bandaranaike Becomes World's First Woman Leader.

Indonesia Severs Relations With Holland.

Republic Of Korea's Former President Syngman Rhee Flees To Hawaii.

A Campaign To Spread The Marxist Theories Of Mao Tse-tung To The Masses Kicks Off In Red China.

Mao Tse-tung

Communist Pathet Lao Invade Northern Laos.

Laos Government Escapes To Cambodia As Vientiane Is Engulfed In War.

Guerrillas Fighting The South Vietnam Diem Regime Form The National Liberation Front Under The Leadership Of Ho Chi Minh.

MIDDLE EAST

The First Border Clashes Since 1958 Break Out Between Israel And Syria.

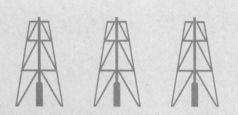

OPEC Is Formed With Iraq, Iran, Kuwait And Saudi Arabia.

In An Historic Meeting Held At New York's Waldorf Astoria Hotel, Israel's Premier David Ben-Gurion And Chancellor Konrad Adenauer Discuss German-Jewish Relations And World Problems.

David Ben-Gurion

Israeli Prime Minister David Ben-Gurion Announces The Israeli Capture In Argentina Of Adolph Eichmann, Notorious World War II Leader Of The Nazi Program For The Extermination Of Jews.

Israel And Argentina Settle Their Dispute Over The Eichmann Kidnapping From Argentina.

IRAN Falls Into Disfavor With Arab League For Its Recognition Of Israel.

CORNERSTONE FOR EGYPT'S ASWAN DAM
Is Laid By President Nasser.

Passings

Long-serving politician **Edith Nourse Rogers**, who spent 35 years in the House of Representatives, dies at age 79.

Lawyer **Joseph N. Welch**, who represented the Army in hearings against Senator Joseph McCarthy and charmed television viewers with his animated courtroom behavior, dies at age 69.

British Rule Ends As Cyprus Becomes A Republic. Cyprus Gains Its Independence.

WHAT A YEAR IT WAS!

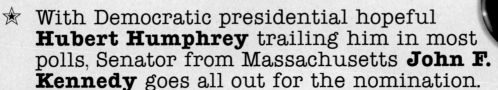

Richard Nixon throws his hat into the presidential ring.

Setting A Campaign Record, **Richard Nixon** Becomes First Candidate To Campaign In All 50 States.

Yo Quiero Vivir En La Casa Blanca

Jacqueline Kennedy campaigns for her husband John's bid for the White House addressing the crowd in Spanish and Italian.

Catholic Presidential Hopeful Senator John F. Kennedy Declares:

"I don't think my religion is anyone's business."

★ With Democratic presidential hopeful **Hubert Humphrey** trailing him in most polls, Senator from Massachusetts **John F. Kennedy** goes all out for the nomination.

★ Following the Kennedy primary victory over Humphrey in Wisconsin, Senator **Robert C. Byrd** of West Virginia heads coalition to stop Kennedy.

★ **Humphrey** withdraws from race.

★ Senator **John F. Kennedy** wins the Democratic nomination for president — names Texas Senator **Lyndon B. Johnson** as V.P.

★ Vice President **Richard M. Nixon** gets the Republican nomination for president becoming the first vice president in the history of the 2-party system to win the presidential nomination and names **Henry Cabot Lodge** as his running mate.

★ Presidential candidates Senator **John F. Kennedy** and Vice President **Richard M. Nixon** clash in their first TV debate.

The CHANGING Of The GUARD

Enthusiastic crowds gather to greet president-elect John F. Kennedy who defeated GOP standard bearer Richard Nixon in one of the closest presidential elections on record.

Jacqueline and John F. Kennedy *(above)* and Patricia and Richard M. Nixon *(below)*.

As America enters the critical and challenging 60's, the youngest man ever elected President of the United States (43) assumes the presidential burdens from the oldest man (70) to ever hold the office.

The CHANGING of The GUARD

At the White House the stage is set for the first meeting between President Eisenhower and Senator Kennedy.

The present and future head of state meet in an atmosphere of cordial informality to discuss the transition from the present to the incoming administration in what is reported to be the most friendly and managed transition of power in history.

The CHANGING of The GUARD

In a meeting that lasts almost three hours and includes some of President Eisenhower's top advisors, the topics, in addition to procedural, include discussion of the responsibilities of world leadership the nation now bears and the problems facing America in the coming months. To the world, both men present a clear picture of national unity in the search for peace as well as in the orderly transfer of the reins of power.

President-Elect Kennedy Names **Dean Rusk** Secretary Of State, **Chester Bowles** Undersecretary Of State, **Robert F. Kennedy** Attorney General And **Adlai E. Stevenson** Ambassador To The United Nations.

Although details of the meeting remain private, Senator Kennedy makes the following statement to the press:

"I want to take this opportunity to express my appreciation to President Eisenhower. He was extremely generous in the time that he gave to the discussion and the problems that the United States now faces and will face in the coming months... The White House will have a statement to make on the meeting shortly."

However you do your rock-and-roll...
you'll need the real thirst-quencher!

The faster the action—the thirstier you get—and the more you need 7-Up! And talk about fast action, wait till you feel 7-Up go to work. With the first sparkling sip, it starts to quench. With the last sparkling sip, thirst is down and out. So when you bring on the fun and games—bring on the 7-Up! It's *always* 7-Up time. Nothing, nothing, **nothing** <u>does it</u> like Seven-Up!

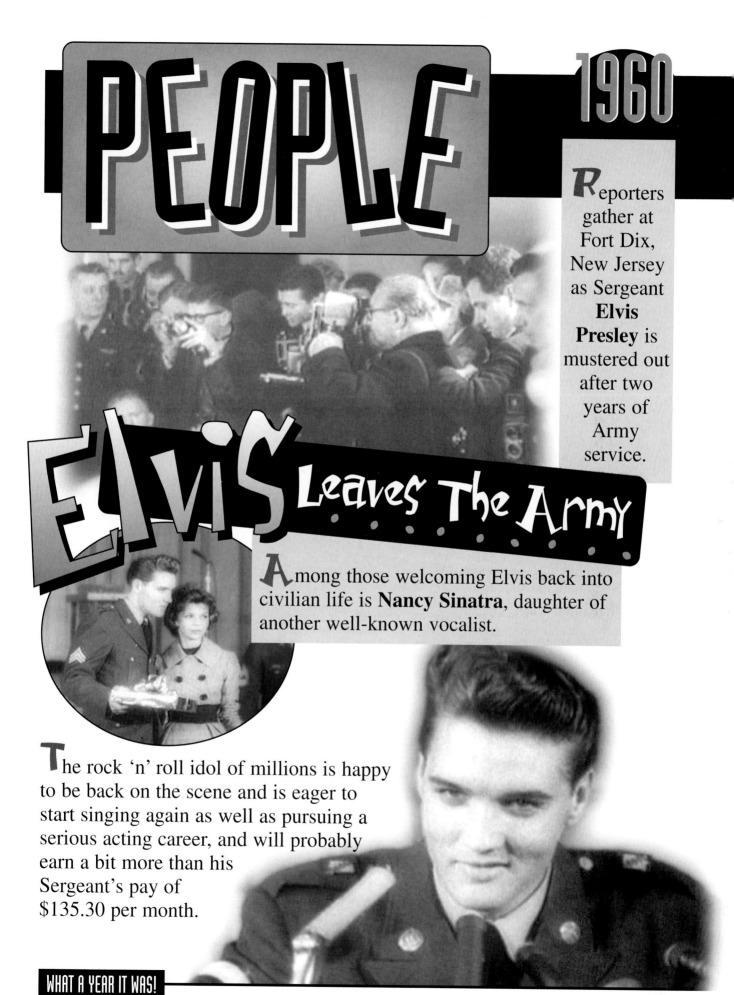

PEOPLE

Reporters gather at Fort Dix, New Jersey as Sergeant **Elvis Presley** is mustered out after two years of Army service.

ELVIS Leaves The Army

Among those welcoming Elvis back into civilian life is **Nancy Sinatra**, daughter of another well-known vocalist.

The rock 'n' roll idol of millions is happy to be back on the scene and is eager to start singing again as well as pursuing a serious acting career, and will probably earn a bit more than his Sergeant's pay of $135.30 per month.

WHAT A YEAR IT WAS!

1960 ROYAL GOINGS ON!

Queen
Elizabeth II

Queen Elizabeth II celebrates her 34th birthday.

Queen Elizabeth II greets 500 British newsmen at an unprecedented royal press reception.

Queen Elizabeth II gives birth to her third child and names him **Andrew**, the first baby born to a reigning British monarch since 1857.

FAMOUS BIRTH

A ROYAL PAIN IN THE...EYE

On biting a royal footman above his eye **Princess Margaret's** favorite lap dog **Johnny**, a small Sealyham, falls into disfavor and is banished from the royal court.

In the first royal wedding to be filmed, Britain's PRINCESS MARGARET *marries* ANTONY ARMSTRONG-JONES.

Buckingham Palace announces QUEEN ELIZABETH II *is giving* PRINCESS MARGARET *and* ANTONY ARMSTRONG-JONES *a mansion on Millionaires Row where they will live rent-free.*

QUEEN ELIZABETH bestows title of EARL OF SNOWDEN *on her sister* MARGARET'S *new husband.*

WHEN KINGS MEET

The King Of Nepal meets the King Of Rock 'n' Roll Elvis Presley on the set of *G.I. Blues* filming in Hollywood.

PRINCESS GRACE is a bit miffed when uninvited guest MARIA CALLAS (36) shows up in Monaco at the Princess' Red Cross Ball draped on the arm of her 54-year old boyfriend ARISTOTLE ONASSIS.

Princess Grace

- The **Duke Of Windsor** Contracts To Write An Article For *McCall's* Magazine On His Influence On Men's Fashions And Their Influence On Him For A Paycheck Of $75,000.

- Actress **Judith Anderson** Becomes Dame Judith In An Investiture Conducted By Queen Elizabeth II At Buckingham Palace.

- Jordan's 24-Year Old **King Hussein** Tries His Hand At Driving A "Go Kart" On An Airfield Near Amman.

- Japan's **Crown Prince Akihito's** Wife, **Princess Michiko,** Gives Birth To A Son.

- In America On A State Visit, **King Frederik IX** And **Queen Ingrid** Of Denmark Arrive In Washington.

Heir to the Iranian throne is born in Tehran to QUEEN FARAH DIBA and SHAH MOHAMMED REZA PAHLAVI.

WHAT A YEAR IT WAS!

America has fallen in love with the
new *Princess* phone

In white, beige, pink, blue and turquoise — attractively priced

it's little !... it's lovely !... it lights !

Small size is one of many reasons why the Princess is so popular. It fits in where you didn't have room for an extension before—on a kitchen counter, a desk or a bedside table.

Graceful styling is another reason why everyone is so charmed by this phone. You can put the Princess anywhere. sure that its lines and the color you choose will blend in beautifully.

Lighted dial. It glows in the dark, and, when you lift the receiver. lights up brightly for easy dialing. To order the Princess, just call our Business Office — or ask your telephone man.

BELL TELEPHONE SYSTEM

1960

Frank Sinatra hires blacklisted writer Albert Maltz to work on the screenplay of his film *"The Execution Of Private Slovik."*

Frank   Duke

Frank Sinatra and John Wayne get into a shoving match in the parking lot of the Moulin Rouge nightclub following a charity event because of the Duke's objection to Sinatra hiring blacklisted writer Albert Maltz.

Accused by Walter Winchell of tilting his head back in order to look better, **CARY GRANT** admits that he does indeed have a double chin.

DEAN MARTIN AND JERRY LEWIS HAVE AN EMOTIONAL REUNION AT THE SANDS HOTEL IN LAS VEGAS — THE FIRST SINCE THE 1956 DISSOLUTION OF THEIR TEAM.

Marilyn Monroe designated alternate delegate to the district meeting of the Democratic Committee of Roxbury, Connecticut.

Playwright **Arthur Miller** predicts that when his wife, sex goddess *Marilyn Monroe*, finishes filming his screenplay, ***The Misfits***, she will be recognized for her acting ability.

SNAKES ALIVE!

While on location filming "The World Of Suzie Wong" Hollywood actor William Holden helps save the life of a man who has a 10-foot python wrapped around his neck.

★ Hollywood Movie Star Brigadier General JIMMY STEWART Reports To The Pentagon For Two Weeks of Reservist Training.

★ The First National Bank Of Holbrook, Arizona Elects BING CROSBY Board Chairman.

★ Wearing White Tie And Tails Dashing DOUGLAS FAIRBANKS, JR. Opens London's First Bowling Alley.

Five-Times Married **Clark Gable** Announces He And His Wife **Kay Spreckels** Are Expecting A Child.

Gable

Audrey Hepburn (31) Gives Birth To Her First Child And The Proud Dad **Mel Ferrer** (43) Is Delighted With His Baby Son, Sean.

· WHAT A YEAR IT WAS!

1960

Louis "Satchmo" Armstrong Denied Entry Into South Africa.

Louis Armstrong Celebrates His 60th Birthday With A Bash At His Home On Long Island.

Oh You Beautiful Doll

Collecting dolls since the 1930's when she was America's Little Darling, Shirley Temple donates over 500 dolls with an estimated worth of $50,000 to a Los Angeles museum.

MEL BLANC Is Elected Mayor Of Pacific Palisades, California.

Hollywood actor PETER LAWFORD, married to Pat Kennedy, of the Kennedy clan, is granted U.S. citizenship in Los Angeles.

An outspoken enemy of Adolph Hitler, *Marlene Dietrich* plans a return visit to West Germany for the first time in 30 years where she anticipates a less than enthusiastic reception.

Infuriated By A Racial Slur Directed At Her While Dining In The Luau Restaurant In Beverly Hills With Her White Husband Lennie Hayton, Beautiful Negro Singer **Lena Horne** Responds By Throwing A Hurricane Lamp, Dishes And Three Ashtrays At The Offending Patron.

Tony Curtis bristles after being lambasted for his bad acting by **David Susskind** on his "Open End" TV program and threatens to punch him in the nose.

A BULL'S EYE

Over-endowed mammary glands don't stop Swedish actress ANITA EKBERG from putting a stop to some annoying Roman photographers as she fights back with a bow and arrows hitting a flash gun, camera and a photographer.

WHAT A YEAR IT WAS!

33

1960

HAPPY BIRTHDAY TO YOU

Nobel Prize winning scientist **Linus Pauling** is rescued after being trapped on a ledge 300 feet above the Pacific.

Refusing to name scientists who petitioned the U.N. in 1958 for a halt to atom testing **Linus Pauling** risks contempt of Congress.

Israeli Prime Minister David Ben-Gurion arrives in U.S. to receive honorary degree from Brandeis University.

France's President **Charles de Gaulle** is honored with a Wall Street ticker tape parade attracting over one million people.

Cuba's rebel hero **FIDEL CASTRO** is greeted by 2,000 cheering people as he arrives at the United Nations.

Former middleweight boxing champ, **ROCKY GRAZIANO**, takes over as president of a Long Island bowling center.

◇ **English novelist W. SOMERSET MAUGHAM celebrates his 86th birthday while visiting Bangkok.**

◇ **Adviser to seven presidents philanthropist BERNARD M. BARUCH reaches his 90th birthday and celebrates at home with his family after work.**

◇ **Celebrating his 85th birthday in Cambridge, poet ROBERT FROST, alluding to John F. Kennedy, predicts that the next president of the U.S. will be coming out of Boston.**

◇ **Former world heavyweight boxing champ JACK DEMPSEY celebrates his 65th birthday with friends who gather in the Broadway restaurant bearing Dempsey's name.**

◇ **At a stag reunion of his former staff, five-star General DOUGLAS MACARTHUR celebrates his 80th birthday.**

HONORS FOR A GRAND OLD SOLDIER

To commemorate the 100th anniversary of U.S.-Japanese relations, the man who conquered and occupied Japan for almost six years, 80-year old General **DOUGLAS MACARTHUR**, receives Japan's highest civil award — the Grand Cordon Of The Order of the Rising Sun.

Born into a pagan Negro tribe, 47-year old **Most Rev. Laurian Rugambwa** of Rutabo, Tanganyika becomes the first native African Cardinal ever appointed.

83-year old cellist **PABLO CASALS** breaks his self-imposed moratorium on performing in the U.S. which began in 1939 when the U.S. recognized Franco's Spain, and consents to play at a $500 a ticket benefit held in David Rockefeller's home for the Pablo Casals International Violincello Competition to be held in Israel.

Danny Thomas named "Catholic Big Brother Of The Year" by the Catholic Big Brothers.

Robert F. Kennedy (34), kid brother of presidential hopeful John, is named Father Of The Year by the National Father's Day Committee.

The Birth Notice Of The Year

Proud parents **John** and **Jackie Kennedy** leave the hospital with **John Fitzgerald Kennedy, Jr.**, soon to be the first baby of the land.

GOING TO THE DOGS

J. Paul Getty, thought to be the world's richest man, throws a combination housewarming and coming-out party for the daughter of one of his friends at his new 16th century Sutton Place mansion in Guildford, England where the privileged class get to dine on caviar, lobster and duck and when those eats are gone, out come the hot dogs.

1936 Olympic track legend **Jesse Owens** receives four duplicate Gold Medals from the German National Olympic Committee 24 years after that historic event — the originals were lost after he loaned them to a Harlem exposition celebrating the advancement of Negroes in the U.S.

LET 'ER RIP

Campaigning Atop A Horse In An Albuquerque Parade, Vice Presidential Hopeful **Lyndon B. Johnson** Finds Himself With Torn Trousers When The Palomino He Is Riding Rears Up On Its Hind Legs.

- **Eleanor Roosevelt, Walter Reuther** and **Norman Thomas** among the celebrities sharing the dais at the Sane Nuclear Policy rally held in New York's Madison Square Garden.

- A committee comprised of producers and theatre operators present retiring *New York Times* drama critic **Brooks Atkinson** with a gold, lifetime pass to all legitimate Broadway theatres.

Beat Poet ALLEN GINSBERG ingests the psychedelic drug psilocybin mushrooms under the supervision of Harvard Professor TIMOTHY LEARY, and calls his friend JACK KEROUAC identifying himself as God.

Charged with 2nd degree perjury, TV quiz show big winner **Charles Van Doren** surrenders in New York along with 16 other winners.

The former subject of a Grand Jury investigation in which he admitted lying about his quiz show activities, **Charles Van Doren** is sworn in as a federal grand juror.

Van Doren

COORS BREWERY HEIR ADOLPH IS KIDNAPPED IN GOLDEN, COLORADO.

PASSINGS

Grand dame of American manners for decades, author and socialite **Emily Post** dies at age 86. Her immense tome *"Etiquette"* is currently in its 89th printing.

Diplomat and happy-go-lucky playboy, **Prince Aly Khan**, 48, dies from injuries sustained in a French auto crash.

John B. Kelly, Sr., Olympic sculling champ, wealthy contractor and Princess Grace's father, dies at age 70.

Special **FBI Agent Melvin Purvis**, who was in charge of the Chicago office when **John Dillinger** was slain, dies by his own hand.

☞ Lana Turner's daughter **Cheryl Crane** (16), a ward of juvenile court after she killed her mother's lover in 1958 with a kitchen knife, is remanded to a county school for problem girls.

☞ U.S. State Department investigates Academy Award winning French actress **Simone Signoret's** background to determine if she has any Communist affiliations.

☞ Writer **Norman Mailer** committed to Bellevue Hospital for observation after stabbing his wife with a 2-inch penknife.

☞ Harlem Congressman **Adam Clayton Powell** is charged with tax fraud and perjury.

☞ Brother of convicted Soviet spy Jack Soble, **Robert Soble** is arrested in Orangeburg, New York on espionage charges.

USA - NO! ITALY - YES!

Still serving a 5-year sentence for income tax evasion, bootlegger/gangster **FRANK COSTELLO** is denied his citizenship appeal by the U.S. Court Of Appeals on the grounds he lied when he was naturalized in 1925 by claiming he was in real estate.

WHAT A YEAR IT WAS!

Citing large divorce settlements as the reason for his financial downfall, crooner **Dick Haymes** files for bankruptcy in New York saying he has only $9 towards the curing of his $522,242 debt.

Davis

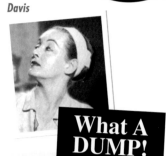

What A DUMP!

Bette Davis is awarded $65,700 in Los Angeles for injuries sustained when she falls down a flight of stairs in a rented house.

An Italian judge grants an annulment of the 1950 Mexican proxy marriage to **Ingrid Bergman** and **Roberto Rossellini**.

Charles Chaplin, Jr. brings a $400,000 malicious libel lawsuit against Hollywood's city fathers for their refusal to put his famous dad on the "Walk Of Fame."

Brando

Marlon Brando's Contempt Charges Against His Ex-Wife Mrs. Marlon Brando (Anna Kashfi) Have Been Dropped And The Actor Is Now Allowed To Have His Son Delivered To His Home Two Afternoons A Week.

$25 Million Is The Amount Of Alimony Being Sought By Marjorie Steele Hartford, 31-Year Old Estranged Wife Of A&P Heir Huntington Hartford.

Sophia Loren and Carlo Ponti go to court in Italy to answer bigamy charges lodged against Ponti on the grounds the Mexican divorce from his first wife is invalid.

Loren

An empty jewel case thought to have held the over $500,000 in jewels stolen from **Sophia Loren** is recovered from the River Thames.

Starring In
MEDICAL ROLES

Suffering from injuries sustained when he trips over a rug in his home, 86-year old Winston Churchill is confined to the hospital bed brought to his home.

For the second time in seven weeks, screen star **Gary Cooper** (59) undergoes major intestinal surgery.

While at work on rewrites for the Broadway-bound musical *Camelot*, Pulitzer Prize winning playwright **Moss Hart** (57) suffers a heart attack.

First Lady **Mamie Eisenhower** Returns Home To The White House After A 3-Week Bout With Acute Asthmatic Bronchitis.

Elvis Presley Breaks The Little Finger On His Right Hand During A Game Of Touch Football On A School Field Near Memphis.

Chico Marx Hospitalized After Suffering Severe Chest Pain While Dining At The Hollywood Friars Club.

HOW WHY YA, HOW WHY YA, HOW WHY YA

Arthur Godfrey has surgery for the removal of a fatty tumor from his back.

French "Sex Kitten" **Brigitte Bardot** Is Recovering In A French Hospital After A Suicide Attempt On Her 26th Birthday.

Shooting of "The Misfits" starring **Marilyn Monroe, Clark Gable, Montgomery Clift** and **Eli Wallach** comes to a stand-still when Marilyn is hospitalized for exhaustion.

the old schnoz ties the knot

after a whirlwind courtship of 16 years, former Copacabana chorus line dancer **Margie Little** arrives at the church to marry boyfriend **Jimmy Durante**.

following the ceremony Jimmy jokes with some of the thousands of fans waiting outside the church all of whom send their best wishes including, we're sure, Mrs. Calabash, wherever you are.

BOBBY DARIN & SANDRA DEE *Tie The Knot*

idols of teenagers across the country actress **Sandra Dee** and singer **Bobby Darin** arrive in Los Angeles to begin a 4-day honeymoon after a midnight wedding in Elizabeth, New Jersey.

The happy couple announced their engagement after completing production in Rome of ***Come September*** co-starring Rock Hudson and Gina Lollobrigida.

WHAT A YEAR IT WAS!

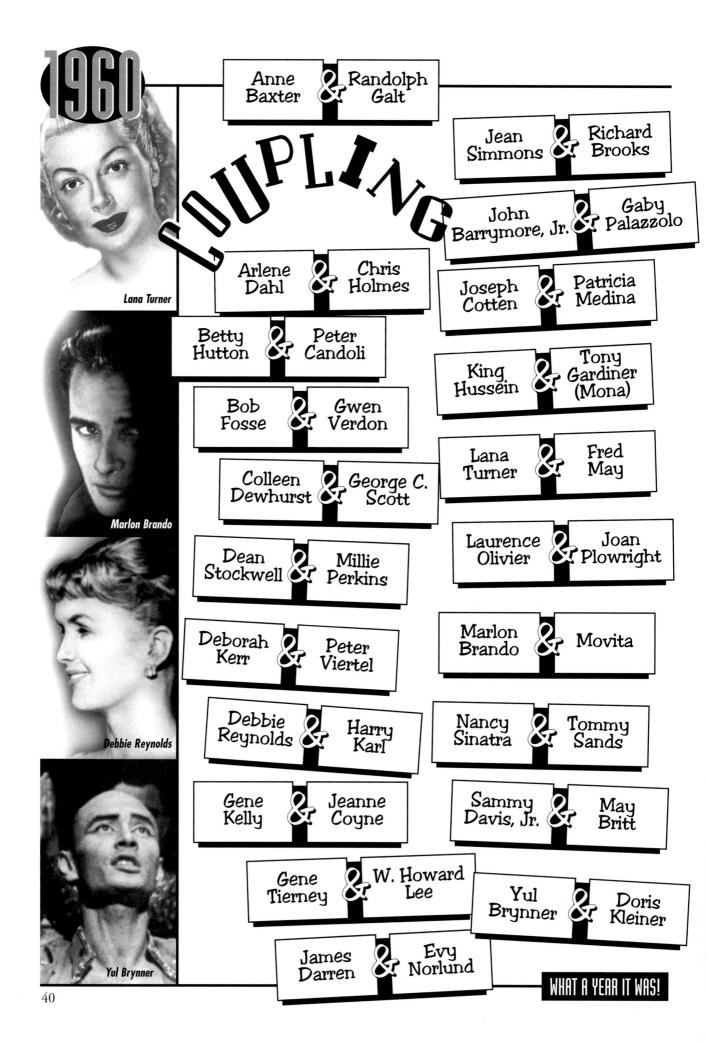

1960

COUPLING

Anne Baxter **&** Randolph Galt

Jean Simmons **&** Richard Brooks

John Barrymore, Jr. **&** Gaby Palazzolo

Arlene Dahl **&** Chris Holmes

Joseph Cotten **&** Patricia Medina

Betty Hutton **&** Peter Candoli

King Hussein **&** Tony Gardiner (Mona)

Bob Fosse **&** Gwen Verdon

Lana Turner **&** Fred May

Colleen Dewhurst **&** George C. Scott

Laurence Olivier **&** Joan Plowright

Dean Stockwell **&** Millie Perkins

Marlon Brando **&** Movita

Deborah Kerr **&** Peter Viertel

Debbie Reynolds **&** Harry Karl

Nancy Sinatra **&** Tommy Sands

Gene Kelly **&** Jeanne Coyne

Sammy Davis, Jr. **&** May Britt

Gene Tierney **&** W. Howard Lee

Yul Brynner **&** Doris Kleiner

James Darren **&** Evy Norlund

Lana Turner

Marlon Brando

Debbie Reynolds

Yul Brynner

WHAT A YEAR IT WAS!

UNCOUPLING

Alan Arkin & Jeremy Yaffe

Jean Simmons & Stewart Granger

Angie Dickinson & Gene Dickinson

Joan Plowright & Roger Gage

Aristotle Onassis & Tina Livanos Onassis

Laurence Olivier & Vivien Leigh

Bette Davis & Gary Merrill

Leo Durocher & Laraine Day

Betty Hutton & Alan W. Livingston

Lucille Ball & Desi Arnaz

Christopher Plummer & Tammy Grimes

Marilyn Monroe & Arthur Miller

Ethel Merman & Robert Six

Shelley Winters & Anthony Franciosa

Fernando Lamas & Arlene Dahl

Willie Nelson & Martha Matthews

Hedy Lamarr & W. Howard Lee

Yul Brynner & Virginia Gilmore

Hedy Lamarr

Laurence Olivier

Vivien Leigh

Marilyn Monroe

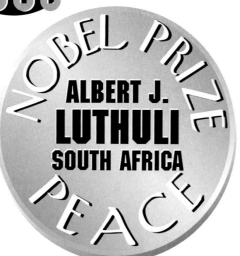

NOBEL PRIZE
ALBERT J. **LUTHULI** SOUTH AFRICA
PEACE

Dick Clark chosen **Grand Marshall** of the **California Beauty Pageant Parade.**

MISS UNIVERSE
Linda Bement,
Salt Lake City, Utah

MISS AMERICA
Lynda Lee Mead,
Natchez, Mississippi

Representing Ohio The First Negro Enters The Miss Universe Contest.

1960 ADVERTISEMENT

No thanks! No calories!

I sweeten with Sucaryl... and weight watching's a pleasure! All the delicious sweetness I crave . . . without adding a single calorie. Tastes better, not bitter. So easy to use in cooking and baking, too. Tablets or liquid, Sucaryl is sold at drugstores everywhere.

Sucaryl®

Abbott Laboratories, North Chicago, Illinois and Montreal, Canada. ®Sucaryl—Abbott's Non-Caloric Sweetener

WHAT A YEAR IT WAS!

POPULAR EX~NEW YORK MAYOR, WILLIAM O'DWYER, RETURNS
TO NEW YORK AFTER LIVING IN MEXICO FOR 10 YEARS ~
TWO OF WHICH HE SPENT AS AMBASSADOR TO MEXICO.

THE WORLD'S TEN MOST GLAMOROUS BACHELORS

The Aga Khan IV, 22

Douglas Burden, 28 (U.S.)

Dick Button, 31 (U.S.)

Crown Prince Constantine, 20 (Greece)

Duke of Kent, 25 (England)

Crown Prince Harald, 23 (Norway)

Prince Raimondo Orsini, 28 (Italy)

Michael Rockefeller, 21 (U.S.)

Toni Sailer, 25 (Austria)

John Fell Stevenson, 24 (U.S.)

THE WORLD'S RICHEST BIDDIES

Ex-Queen Wilhelmina
(The Netherlands)

The Begum
(Widow Of Aga Khan III)

Mrs. Dorothy Killam
(Widow of American businessman
Izaak Walton Killam)

Suzanne Volterra (French Widow)

Queen Elizabeth II (England)

18th Duchess Of Alba (Spain)

Nina Caroline Studley-Herbert, Countess Of Seafield
(Second Richest In England After The Queen)

Sumati Morarjee (India)

VOTE FOR YOUR FAVORITE FLAVOR
IN THE NATIONAL JELL-O ELECTION

National JELL-O Election now in progress at grocery stores throughout the United States. No joke. You are automatically registered and eligible to vote if you can make an "X." So go to the polls in droves. Go in cars. Walk. But go and vote. Vote early; vote often for your favorite JELL-O flavor in the NATIONAL JELL-O ELECTION. Polls close Saturday, October 8.

Jell-O is a registered trade-mark of General Foods Corp.

44

The Brits Do Their Air Thing

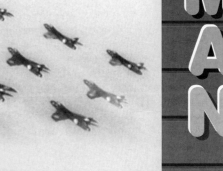

Britain's ace team of precision aerial acrobats take off in tight formation for a stirring demonstration of superb airmanship.

At sonic speeds they perform a dazzling routine of combat maneuvers mixed with outstanding showmanship in which their Hawker Hunter jets are often separated by precarious margins.

Known as "Black Arrows" this team is the pride of the Royal Air Force, second to none in their skills, split-second reactions, iron nerves and a flair for the dramatic.

This crack team ends their routine with a brilliant flourish in the sky.

1960

what price beauty?

the food and drug administration approves a new dye to give florida oranges a deeper color so they can compete with the more beautiful california oranges.

An Oral Contraceptive Pill For Public Consumption Receives FDA Approval.

NO MORE RHYTHM THEN BLUES

A study conducted in Texas reveals that birth control is as popular with Catholics as with Jews and Protestants.

The Boy Scouts Of America Celebrates Its 50th Anniversary.

$105 Buys The Full-Scale Model Of A Do-It-Yourself **Fallout Shelter** Displayed In A New York Bank.

The First Outdoor **Telephone Booths** Installed In New York City.

F.A.O. Schwarz, The "Tiffany Of The Toy World," Offers Discounted Merchandise For The First Time In Its 98 Years Of Being In Business.

Unaware That The War Has Ended, A Japanese Soldier Is Found After 16 Years Of Hiding Out In The Jungles Of Guam.

DICK TRACY

Celebrates His 30th Year Of Being In The Comics.

The Salvation Army Celebrates Its **80th** Anniversary.

WHAT A YEAR IT WAS!

LATKES & LEIS

HAWAII
Gets Its First Jewish Temple.

A 5-Year Program To Feed The Hungry Is Inaugurated By The Food And Agricultural Organization.

THE STRIPES AND A FEW MORE STARS

Americans Across The Country Celebrate Independence Day By Flying The New 50-Star Flag For The First Time Which Reflects The Admittance Of Hawaii Into The Union.

In an unprecedented decision the **Mississippi Supreme Court** rules that it is *mandatory for parents to send their children to college if they are financially able and the child is college material.*

U.S. Supreme Court *refuses to look into government plan to spray DDT.*

The U.S. Supreme Court holds that *evidence seized by state officers in violation of the fourth amendment of the Constitution is inadmissible* overturning the "Silver Platter Doctrine."

New York City schoolteachers *go on strike* for higher pay leaving classrooms unattended.

Student enrollment in the U.S. reaches an *all-time high of 48,650,000.*

A poll conducted by U.S. census takers reveals *one out of ten adult Americans is functionally illiterate* spurring the nation's first mass TV assault on illiteracy by presenting educational programs geared expressly toward teaching reading and writing.

✝ **National Council of Churches** attacks programming containing *sex and violence* on television and radio.

1960

A White House Report Indicates That American Children Are Getting Too Fat.

GO NORTH, EAST, SOUTH OR WEST YOUNG MAN

John F. Kennedy proposes creating a **Peace Corps** comprised of young Americans who will go into underdeveloped nations to assist in improving living standards.

The oldest person to ever serve in Congress, Democratic Senator from Rhode Island **Theodore Francis Green**, retires at 92.

The nation's first SMOG CONTROL BILL is approved by the California legislature.

1960

U.S. POPULATION:
179,323,175

California is the fastest growing state in the United States followed by **Florida, New York, Texas, Ohio, Michigan, Illinois, New Jersey, Pennsylvania** and **Maryland**.

Where The Grass Is Greener

Approximately one-third of the nation is moving to the suburbs.

Over a third of the nation's population resides in U.S. urban centers with a population of a million or more people.

HOW YOU GONNA KEEP THEM DOWN ON THE FARM

For The First Time In History Less Than 10% Of The Nation's Population Lives On Farms.

TEN MOST POPULATED U.S. CITIES

New York, New York
Chicago, Illinois
Los Angeles, California
Philadelphia, Pennsylvania
Detroit, Michigan
Baltimore, Maryland
Houston, Texas
Cleveland, Ohio
Washington, D.C.
St. Louis, Missouri

Over $11,000,000,000 is spent on highway development throughout the United States.

ATTENTION SHOPPERS!

Portland, Oregon is site of **LARGEST SHOPPING CENTER IN THE U.S.** — the $100 million Lloyd Center.

Southern California experiences its **Coldest Night In 10 Years** with temperatures dropping to 12 degrees in the Santa Monica Mountains.

MEMBERSHIP IN 4-H Clubs OF AMERICA REACHES A RECORD HIGH OF 2,301,722.

STILL FASTER THAN THE U.S. POST OFFICE

Nevada's governor and lieutenant governor assist in delivering the mail during a reenactment of the Pony Express in celebration of its centennial.

Plans Are Announced To Build A New $38,000,000 **Madison Square Garden Sports And Entertainment Center** On The West Side Of Manhattan.

The Downtown-Lower Manhattan Association Headed By David Rockefeller Unveils $250 Million Proposal For **World-Trade And Financial Center.**

ALONG FOR THE RIDES

Freedomland Amusement Park Opens In New York City.

WHAT A YEAR IT WAS!

49

In The Worst Race Riots To Hit Mississippi Ten People Are Shot In Biloxi When Negroes Try To Swim At The Restricted "Whites Only" Beaches.

Dr. Martin Luther King, Jr.

■ **Negro students quietly seek service** at a Woolworth store lunch counter in Greensboro, North Carolina sparking protest sit-ins throughout the south.

■ **Police arrest Negro sit-in protesters** in Atlanta, Georgia and Orangeburg, South Carolina.

■ **Nashville integrates six lunch counters** — the first in the south.

■ **Segregated lunch counters** in 100 southern cities in the Woolworth, Kress, W.T. Grant and McCrory-McLellan store chains are now integrated.

Charged with perjury stemming from the Alabama bus boycott, Martin Luther King, Jr. is arrested in Atlanta.

Martin Luther King, Jr. is acquitted of perjury charges growing out of the 1956 bus boycott.

On parole for a traffic violation, Reverend Martin Luther King, Jr. is arrested at Atlanta sit-in on grounds it violated his parole.

Robert F. Kennedy discusses Martin Luther King, Jr.'s imprisonment with his wife, Coretta.

Muslim Leader **Elijah Muhammed** Calls For An American Negro State In The United States Or Africa At A Rally Held In New York.

First Negroes enrolled in white schools in Roanoke, Virginia.

Once the country's largest segregated school district, a Negro boy enters first grade in a white school in Houston, Texas.

It's graduation day from Little Rock's Central High School for Carlotta Walls and Jefferson Thomas, two of the seven Negroes who were escorted by U.S. paratroops into the previously all-white school in 1957.

- The former Confederate Capitol Building in Montgomery, Alabama is the site where 1,000 Negro students gather to pray and sing the national anthem.
- Fayette County, Tennessee is the target of a U.S. Justice Department lawsuit to cease and desist the use of economic pressures including eviction notices against Negroes who register to vote.
- Nerve gas is used on students picketing the White House in protest over racial segregation.
- AFL-CIO supports Negro boycotts.

NEVER AGAIN, WE HOPE!

A rash of anti-Semitic acts break out worldwide from West Germany to the United States smearing synagogues, public buildings and Jewish homes with swastikas.

BOMB EXPLODES AT HOME OF CARLOTTA WALLS, ONE OF THE NEGROES AT CENTRAL HIGH IN LITTLE ROCK.

WHITE YOUTHS IN HOUSTON BEAT NEGRO WITH CHAINS AND CARVE SIX "K's" IN HIS CHEST.

WHAT A YEAR IT WAS!

FBI Director J. Edgar Hoover proposes the x-raying of airline passengers' baggage in an effort to prevent bombings on airplanes as well as the installation in cockpits of fire-proof tape recorders to record conversations between crew and pilots which could be used in determining the cause of crashes.

DIPLOMATIC IMMUNITY OUR FOOT

In the biggest narcotics bust ever made by the U.S. Bureau of Narcotics, **MAURICIO ROSAL,** Guatemala's Ambassador to Belgium, is arrested along with three black leather valises containing 110 pounds of pure unadulterated heroin with a street value of over $20 million.

A HUNG JURY

The jury couldn't make up its mind in the sensational trial of **Dr. Bernard Finch** and his girl-friend, **Carole Tregoff**, indicted for the murder of the good doctor's wife, so a second trial is scheduled.

UNEXPECTED STAY OF EXECUTION GRANTED TO CARYL CHESSMAN BY CALIFORNIA GOVERNOR EDMUND G. BROWN.

AFTER RECEIVING 8 STAYS OF EXECUTION DATING BACK TO 1948 AND 10 YEARS ON DEATH ROW, CARYL CHESSMAN IS FINALLY EXECUTED IN SAN QUENTIN.

Protestors against HUAC investigations into alleged Communist activities arrested in San Francisco.

THE FBI

Issues Posters **WARNING MOTORISTS** Against Picking Up Hitchhikers.

You Call This A Tip?–Bang! Bang!

With Over 500 Of New York's 30,000 Cabbies Held Up Last Year, United Taxi Owners Guild Lobby For Permission To Allow **Cab Drivers** To Carry Guns.

19 Mafia delegates to Apalachin meeting sentenced to prison terms of up to five years.

WE AIN'T NO CROOKS

Alleged underworld leaders arrested at Apalachin, New York in 1957 have conspiracy convictions reversed by U.S. Court Of Appeals on grounds of insufficient evidence.

In testimony given before the U.S. House Subcommittee on Legislative Oversight, DICK CLARK denies accepting "payola" from record companies as an enticement to play their recordings.

GUILTY VERDICT UP IN SMOKE

"The King Of Torts" attorney MELVIN BELLI fails to establish a legal precedent that a tobacco company can be held liable for a smoker's death by lung cancer when he loses a lawsuit against Liggett & Myers and R.J. Reynolds brought against these companies by a widow whose husband died of lung cancer. The Louisiana jury rules there is no proof smoking causes cancer.

TEEN CORNER

CHEATING

You're a creep if you report someone.

EXCESSIVE DRINKING

Boys think it's ok to experiment and to see what it feels like to get high but excessive drinking is something to be ashamed of.

PICKING UP BOYS

Most girls don't feel comfortable going out with someone they don't know and if they do, feel ashamed if the boy tries to get fresh with them.

SARCASM OR TEASING

Most teenagers don't like to see someone's feelings get hurt and feel ashamed if they are responsible for making someone feel bad.

STEALING

Not acceptable and they do not feel obliged to cover for someone who has stolen.

FOLLOWING ARE ACCEPTABLE ETHICS "VIOLATIONS" BECAUSE THE RESTRICTIONS ARE CONSIDERED "DUMB"

LYING ABOUT ONE'S AGE IN ORDER TO:

- *Get into a movie without an adult;*
- *Purchase cigarettes;*
- *Purchase alcoholic beverages;*
- *Get into a nightclub;*
- *Use forged ID to accomplish any of the above.*

HEY DAD, HOW ABOUT A COKE WITH A CHOCOLATE MALTED CHASER

A nationwide survey of 933 teenagers reveals that drinking is much lower and less frequent than believed and that the strongest influence is the example set by parents — if they drink their children are apt to drink.

WHAT A YEAR IT WAS!

DATING & MARRIAGE
TIPS FOR TEENAGERS

 1960

- Make sure your parents like your date.
- Discuss your engagement or marriage plans with your parents.
- Know the difference between love and infatuation. *(true love allows time for planning your marriage)*
- Be realistic about your expectations from marriage.
- Don't mistake a *"smooth dancer"* for marriage material.
- Marriage is not a road to happiness unless you are happy already.
- Look for signs of personality disorders that could adversely affect your marriage.
- Avoid premarital sex relations.
- Discuss your mutual feelings, plans and hopes for the future.
- Watch out for someone who bickers with everyone as that could be what you will have to look forward to in your marriage.
- Don't expect any annoying personality traits to disappear after you marry.
- Make sure you agree on your friends and recreational activities.
- Don't avoid discussions about important issues.
- Marry within your age range.
- If an individual doesn't have a good set of ethics, adjusting to the conventions of married life could be difficult.

Trying To Tie The Knot?
Best Places To Find A Husband:
- **School**
- **Parties**
- **Office**

Ideal age for a man to marry is between 22 and 30 and for a girl between 20 and 28.

- Courtship should last at least two years followed by a short engagement since about one-third of all first engagements are broken and a longer engagement period would allow for the surfacing of "irreconcilable differences."
- If you are lucky enough to find your man he'll probably propose to you in his car.
- After you finally get married, you might experience some difficult times somewhere between the fifth to ninth years.

Before You Say Yes, Make Sure He:

- Works in a field you respect;
- Cares about what other people think of him;
- Accepts women as equals;
- Is responsible;
- Manages money well;
- Wants to be married;
- Is considerate of strangers;
- Has nice friends;
- Is pleasing in his behavior;
- Likes your friends and family;
- Has similar religious views;
- Shares a few basic interests;
- Treats you with consideration.

While more girls than boys graduate high school, only 35% of them go on to college.

IN SEARCH OF THE
PERFECT FACE & FIGURE
(A Poll Conducted At The University of Wisconsin Reveals Student Wish List)

GIRLS
7 Pounds Lighter
Smaller Nose
Shorter
Slimmer Hips
Smaller Waist
Bigger Busts
Bigger Eyes
More Oval Face

BOYS
Smaller Nose
Smaller Ears
More Prominent Chin
Weigh A Bit More
Taller

WHAT COLLEGE MEN & WOMEN WANT FROM THEIR SWEETIES

WOMEN WANT:
Someone to look up to
Strong mind
Dominant character
Strong physically
Help with important decisions
Respect their ideals

MEN WANT:
Someone who gives them self confidence
Understands their moods
Encourage their ambitions

HOW WE SPEND OUR DAY
(according to a professor at University of Michigan)

Writing:	9%
Reading:	16%
Speaking:	30% (120-160 words per minute)
Listening:	45%
Listening Attention Span:	2-3 Seconds
Thinking:	300 to 800 words per minute

YES, BUT
CAN SHE TYPE?

According to a recent survey of 500 employment agencies around the **U.S.** skills and appearance are almost neck in neck in determining who lands the job and here's what the female applicant should wear on her interview:

- **Suit or Dress** (conservative color)
- **Small Hat**
- **Gloves**
- **Little or No Jewelry**
- **Light Make-Up**
- **Tidy Hair Style**
- **(wear deodorant, of course and carry a small clothes brush)**

WHAT A YEAR IT WAS!

SQUARE-MEAL SANDWICHES
You make 'em with meat - Armour Star! ★

1960

Anne Frank's house in Amsterdam where she and her family were hidden from the Nazis during World War II is being restored as a memorial to the heroic Jewish teenager who died in a concentration camp. *"The Diary Of Anne Frank"* fulfilled her dream of becoming a famous writer.

An article printed in the Soviet newspaper <u>Izvestia</u> indicates that most Russian professional specialists are women.

In Rome,
Pope John XXIII holds the first synod or diocesan ecclesiastical council to define the fundamental laws that will effect the Catholic Church worldwide including rules for tightening discipline for both clergy and laity including forbidding priests to smoke in public or attend plays or films, and for Roman women, sacraments will be denied if they have bare arms or wear men's clothing.

The **United Nations** Celebrates Its **15th** Anniversary.

- Swiss women granted right to vote in municipal elections.

- U.S. industrialist **Cyrus S. Eaton** recipient of the Soviet Union's Lenin Peace Prize.

In Response To The Communist Government's **Policy On** Collectivization, **East** German Refugees Flock To **West Berlin**.

OVER *15 Million* World War II **Refugees** REMAIN UNSETTLED Fifteen Years After **The War** With The *Oldest* Refugee Being *105* Years Old.

Red Cross Report Documenting TORTURE IN ALGERIA Published By The French Newspaper Le Monde.

QUEEN ELIZABETH II LAUNCHES BRITAIN'S FIRST NUCLEAR SUBMARINE.

ITALY SUCCESSFULLY TESTS THE LEONARDO DA VINCI WHICH AT 32,000 TONS IS THE LARGEST OCEAN LINER BUILT SINCE WORLD WAR II.

WHAT A YEAR IT WAS!

1960

UNDER THE CITY BY THE SEA

Plans are completed for the construction of railroad tunnels under San Francisco Bay that would connect San Francisco and Oakland, California.

CRUMPETS & CREPES

Great Britain and France explore the possibilities of building a Channel tunnel that would link their two railway systems.

A DAMMING EXPERIENCE

In ceremonies at Aswan, Egypt, construction of Aswan High Dam is officially underway.

- Mexico and U.S. to build Rio Grande Dam.
- The U.S. and Canada agree to joint venture in building a hydroelectric plant on the Columbia River.
- Vienna is site of Fourth International Atomic Energy Agency Conference.
- Construction of a 17.5-mile bridge and tunnel crossing lower Chesapeake Bay begins.

CRUISING DOWN THE RIVER

The St. Lawrence Seaway extending from Montreal to Lake Ontario is completed at a cost of around $441,600,000.

A BRIDGE TOO FAR

A 21-mile bridge that would link South Foreland, near Dover, England and Calais, France is being explored by American, British and French companies.

THEM BONES, THEM BONES, THEM THIGH BONES

A fossil discovered in Mexico is 30,000 years old indicating man lived in the Western Hemisphere 20,000 years earlier than previously thought.

NOT JUST ANOTHER PRETTY MAMMAL

Marine scientist John C. Lily reports that a five-year study reveals the bottle-nosed dolphin has a brain equal to or superior to humans with intelligence as high or possibly higher. With highly developed communication skills, they mimic human sounds, help rescue each other in distress and have a good sense of humor.

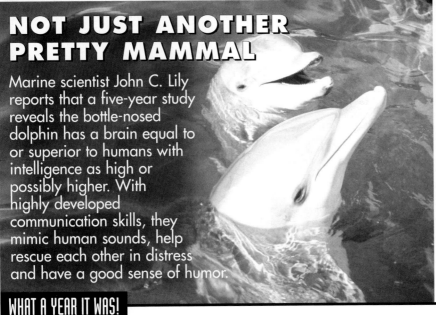

Well Preserved Parchment Scrolls Discovered By Israeli Archeologists Containing 16 Verses From The Book Of Exodus.

WHAT A YEAR IT WAS!

57

1960

UP, UP & AWAY

Veteran aviatrix **Jacqueline Cochran** becomes first woman to fly at **Mach 2** (twice the speed of sound).

WINNER: The Tenth Annual All Women's International Air Race: **Mrs. Edna Gardner Whyte**, Fort Worth, Texas who flies a Cessna 120 from Miami to San Salvador, a distance of 2,498 miles, in 20 hours, 20 minutes, 20 seconds.

NO MORE SLIP SLIDING AWAY

First heavy transport plane equipped with skis touches down at Byrd Station Base in Antarctica.

Boeing 707 service inaugurated by Sabena Airlines.

The 101st Airborne Division at Fort Campbell, Kentucky is first to receive the Army's newest weapon—the M14—which replaces several weapons including the famous M1 Garand.

The new Convair 880, with a cruising speed of 615 m.p.h. sets new commercial record on a round-trip flight from New York's Idlewild Airport to New Orleans.

FASTER THAN A SPEEDING EVERYTHING

In two separate flights, the **X-15 Rocket Plane** sets record for flying higher and faster than any manned plane in history reaching a height of 136,000 ft. piloted by Major Robert White and pilot Joseph A. Walker reaches speed of 2,196 m.p.h.

P A S S I N G

The first female pilot in America, **Ruth Rowland Nichols** dies at age 59.

ALONE, OH SO ALL ALONE

Winner of the one-man boat race across the Atlantic Ocean is 59-year old British adventurer **Francis Chichester** making the crossing in 40 days—16 less than the previous westbound transatlantic record.

AN EASY, FUN WAY TO BREAK YOUR BODY PARTS

Trampoline centers, where for $.40 a half-hour you can jump up and down to your heart's content or until something snaps, spring up across the country with such names as *Launching Pad, Jumperoo, Tumbling Town* and *Bunny Hop*.

First ascent of Mt. Everest from the northern side is achieved by a Communist Chinese team.

New Zealand's famed mountaineer SIR EDMUND HILLARY ends his three-month Himalayan search for the Abominable Snowman without tracking down the legendary Yeti.

WHAT A YEAR IT WAS!

LET'S CUT THE CRINKLE

A member of the British cabinet appeals to manufacturers to come up with a candy wrapper that doesn't make noise so that theatre audiences won't be disturbed by the sound of candy being unwrapped.

NOT AN ORGY IN SIGHT

Allen Vincent-Barwood, former Canadian frogman and currently professor at the American University of Beirut in Lebanon, and his partner, New Yorker **Melvin Rizzi**, decide to take the plunge into the Dead Sea in search of Sodom and Gomorrah but find no traces of the cities of sin.

SOMETHING TO STEW ABOUT

Editor of the ***Northern District Health Quarterly*** suggests for those people tired of the traditional break-fast of bacon and eggs, cereal or pancakes they might try a cheeseburger or stew for a change.

the latest word from a london researcher is that a wife who works definitely helps improve her marriage.

The NEW YORK TIMES begins mailing its Sunday Edition in plastic bags.

DON'T MESS WITH THE METER MAID BABES

100 women making up a unit known as **"Meter Maids"** hit the streets of New York armed with citation books and the authority to issue warnings and summonses for violations.

GOLD REACHES A RECORD $40.60 AN OUNCE ON THE LONDON MARKET — U.S. PRICE STAYS AT $35 AN OUNCE.

A Topanga, California school-teacher goes on trial on nine charges of professional misconduct including calling one of her students stupid.

Three Major Lutheran Denominations Merge Forming The American Lutheran Church In Minneapolis.

New York developer William Zeckendorf sells his majority interest in 11,000 acres in the Santa Monica Mountains to a group of eastern developers making it one of the largest land deals in recent Southern California history.

SOMETHING TO ROAR ABOUT

A new children's zoo is going to be constructed in Central Park thanks to a donation of $500,000 by New York's Democratic ex-Governor and Senator Herbert H. Lehman, 82, and his wife Edith, in honor of their 50th wedding anniversary.

HEY BIG SPENDER

Mrs. James R. McManus, a Mill Valley housewife, creates Charge Accounts Anonymous to help women get their urge to charge under control.

WHERE'S A JERK WHEN YOU NEED ONE?

With the salary of a good soda jerk becoming too high for most drugstores, only 60% of the nation's 53,000 pharmacies still have soda fountains.

WHAT A YEAR IT WAS!

NEW WORDS &

ALTERNATING GRADIENT SYNCHROTRON
A mighty atom smasher.

CURTAIN-HOPPER
One who visits Iron Curtain countries.

AMERICAN FOOTBALL LEAGUE
A football league in competition with the National Football League.

DIALYSER
A synthetic kidney.

DYNAPOLIS
A planned town, with an eye towards future growth, including self-contained neighborhoods.

ANCHORMAN
A television host.

BEATNIKO
A university student trying to behave like a beatnik.

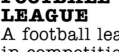

FEE-VEE
Television programming that costs money to watch.

FIDELISTA
A believer in Fidel Castro and his doctrine.

BEDBUG
A fraudulent financial offering.

CHICKEN SWITCH
The cancel switch in weapons.

GAWKOCRACY
Name for television viewers.

GROWTHMAN
A person supporting financial growth.

BLUEGRASS
A traditional type of music akin to country, created by Bill Monroe of Kentucky, the Bluegrass State.

JUNIOR JET SET
Gaudy adolescents.

KNEEL-IN
Negroes who demonstrate against racial discrimination by attending white-only churches.

CLIFFHANGER
An organization that can stop its own demise.

COSMONAUT
A Russian astronaut.

CLOSED ECOLOGICAL SYSTEM
A closed living environment, such as a spaceship.

EXPRESSIONS

LASER
Acronym for Light Amplification by Stimulated Emission of Radiation.

MOLECULAR ELECTRONICS
Electronics that use parts of molecules in various inventions.

NORTH-VISION
A television network in Northern Europe.

SHOUT SHOP
An ad firm on Manhattan's Madison Avenue.

OFFICING
Finding and organizing a group of business suites.

SIT-IN
Negroes who defy custom and/or law and sit at an all-white establishment.

OMNISTRAIN
The pressures of living in the contemporary world.

PLUGOLA
A form of marketing which mentions merchandise on television and radio shows.

SITTER
An individual Negro protester who sits at a segregated restaurant.

ROYOLA
Royalties earned from records entangled in the payola scandal.

RANGER
A transport made of rockets.

SQUIRCH
A term meaning squirm and wince.

TALK-UP
A dialogue.

RECYCLING
A way to turn human waste into food or water.

VALANCE HEATING SYSTEM
A heating system which utilizes a room's valance.

SCRAMBLE CAFETERIA
A cafeteria set up with separate sections so patrons can avoid waiting in one long line.

 WILD CARD RULE
A football rule allowing a different player to enter the game between plays.

SCROLLERY
Searching for ancient scrolls.

When you're not feeling really appreciated, have a cup of tea; most cheerful stuff in the world. Try drinking tea with your evening meal for a week; see if the world doesn't look a little brighter. Tea psyches you up.

TAKE TEA AND SEE

To get the most out of tea — make it hefty, hot and hearty. Use one teaspoon or one tea bag per cup. Add bubbly, boiling water and brew 3 to 5 minutes. For instant tea, follow directions on the package.

BUSINESS

MEDIAN FAMILY INCOME FOR FAMILY OF FOUR:

$6,300.

THE HIGHEST NOVEMBER UNEMPLOY- MENT SINCE 1940 IS AT

6.3%

ACCORDING TO THE U.S. LABOR DEPARTMENT.

ACCORDING TO A GOVERNMENT SURVEY, A COLLEGE EDUCATION ADDS $100,000 TO A MAN'S LIFETIME EARNINGS.

THE AVERAGE PAID- HOLIDAY BENEFIT AMOUNTS TO 7 DAYS A YEAR.

U.S. NATIONAL DEBT AT THE END OF FISCAL 1960: $286,331,000,000.

CONRAD HILTON Opens His 41st Hotel In Denver.

ALLSTATE INSURANCE ANNOUNCES PLANS TO INTRODUCE CANCEL-PROOF AUTO INSURANCE.

THERE'S A WHOLE LOT OF CHARGING GOING ON

Number Of
Credit Card Holders

Diners Club
1.1 Million

Carte Blanche
400,000

American Express
750,000

J.C. Penney Announces A Departure From Its "Cash Only" Policy

Anticipating Setting Up Charge Account Service In Approximately 600 Of Its 1,687 Stores By Next Year.

Race tracks are ordered by the **IRS** to report all winners of $600 or more to insure payment of taxes.

Douglas Aircraft Celebrates The 40th Anniversary Of Its First Plane.

WHAT A YEAR IT WAS!

63

CHOO CHOOS STOP CHUGGING

Trainmen on the Long Island Railroad bring operations to a screeching halt for 25 days as they strike primarily for five-day work week.

In accordance with the Railway Labor Act, a 3-man emergency board is set up by President Eisenhower to investigate a dispute between the major railroads and 11 non-operating railroad unions.

Michael J. Quill, president of the Transport Workers Union, calls a Labor Day weekend strike shutting down the nation's biggest rail carrier — the Pennsylvania Railroad.

Racial qualifications for membership eliminated by the Brotherhood Of Railroad Trainmen.

Representing 1.5 million workers, the Negro Labor Council is organized in Detroit by A. Philip Randolph, president of the Brotherhood Of Sleeping Car Porters.

More than 400 members of Local 533 of the International Brotherhood Of Teamsters stage a strike at one of the busiest airports in the world—New York's Idlewild International Airport.

DRIVERS, DRIVERS EVERYWHERE, SEARCHING FOR TRAINS THAT AREN'T THERE

An estimated 300,000 Boston commuters are forced to drive to work when public transportation workers call a wildcat strike.

THE SHOW DOESN'T GO ON

A contract dispute between the Actors Equity Association and the League of New York Theatres closes down Broadway theatres for the first time since 1919.

CANNERY MEN CAN CANNING THE CANS

Unable to reach an agreement with the Processors and Growers Association, 10,000 members of the Cannery Workers Union go on strike in Northern California.

Boycotts and strikes to be employed by the Amalgamated Clothing Workers Of America in protest over low-cost clothing being imported from Japan and other cheap labor countries.

John L. Lewis
Resigns As President Of The United Mine Workers Of America.

John L. Lewis

Before you buy the new Royal Electric Typewriter, please do yourself, your secretary, and your company this service: try all the makes of electric typewriters. Try them for touch, for printwork, for any feature you wish. Only in this way can you really know the worth of the choice you will make.

THE TOP TEN COMPANIES WITH THE LARGEST NUMBER OF SHAREHOLDERS:

American Telephone & Telegraph

General Motors

Standard Oil (N.J.)

General Electric

U.S. Steel

Ford Motor Co.

Socony Mobil Oil

E.I. du Pont de Nemours

Bethlehem Steel

Columbia Gas System

The **Dow-Jones** Reaches A **Record High** Of **685**.

The New York Stock Exchange Reports The Highest Level Of New Common Stocks For Any One Year In Its History.

❒ Registration of the National Stock Exchange Inc. receives approval from U.S. Securities And Exchange Commission making it the third New York City stock exchange and the 14th U.S. Stock Exchange.

❒ New York Stock Exchange expels Anton E. Homsey, a partner in the Boston firm of DuPont, Homsey & Co., for fraudulent acts which endangered a member firm's financial position. This is the first member to be expelled in 22 years.

❒ For the first time in New York Stock Exchange history, bilked customers of DuPont, Homsey & Co. are offered $690,000 to compensate for their losses due to the Boston brokerage firm's misuse of their securities.

It is revealed that **Aristotle Socrates Onassis** controls more than 50% of the Societe des Bains de Mer de Monaco, owners of the Monte Carlo Casino, five hotels and land.

TOP FIVE STOCKS HELD BY THE 75 BIGGEST MUTUAL FUNDS

IBM
Texaco
U.S. Steel
General Electric
Minnesota Mining & Mfg.

WHAT A YEAR IT WAS!

this was the price that was

UNDER $1.00

Ballpoint Pen	$ .05
Paper Napkins	.09
Battery	.20
Tissue	.29
Bleach, 1/2 gal.	.33

Aspirin, 100	$ .49
Detergent	.64
Hair Brush	.79
Cold Cream	.98

FOOD FAVORITES

Applesauce, 15 oz.	$ .10
Avocado, ea.	.07
Bananas, lb.	.10
Bread, loaf	.21
Broccoli, lb.	.12
Butter, lb.	.69
Cantaloupe, lb.	.09
Cheddar Cheese, lb.	.65
Coffee, lb.	.59
Corn, ear	.05
Cottage Cheese, pt.	.23
Cucumbers, lb.	.10
Eggs, dz.	.43
Ice Cream, 1/2 gal.	.59
Ketchup, 12 oz.	.19
Lettuce, head	.05
Milk, qt.	.26

Oranges, lb.	$ .09
Peanut Butter, 16 oz.	.39
Sara Lee Pound Cake	.79
Strawberries, bskt.	.25
Sugar, lb.	.10
Tomatoes, lb.	.10
Watermelon, lb.	.06

LA TOILETTE

Burma Shave	$ .89
Chanel no. 5, spray	5.00
False Eyelashes	2.00
Haircut & Permanent at Bloomingdale's	9.90
Lipstick	1.50
Mascara	2.00
Pan-Cake Make-Up	1.75

MADAME

Bra	$ 3.95
Canvas Sneakers	3.59
Cardigan	12.95
Chiffon Dress w/underslip	10.98
Gucci Handbag	32.00
Pillbox Hat	7.00
Seamless Nylons	1.65
Shoes	8.95-14.95
Silk Crepe Dress, Christian Dior	185.00
Wool Suit	29.95

Home, Sweet Home

Brooklyn, NY, 2 br. house	$ 15,990
Chicago, IL, 3 br. house	21,000
Santa Monica, CA, 3 br. house	23,500
New York, NY, 2 br. Park Avenue coop	45,000
Beverly Hills, CA, 4 br. house w/pool	156,500

MONSIEUR

Dress Shirt	$ 3.95
Loafers	10.95
Silk Ties	1.99
Slacks	4.98
Wool Suit	79.50

ON THE ROAD AGAIN...

Volkswagen	$ 1,675.00
Chevy Corvair	2,038.00
One-Way Airfare from L.A. to New York or Hawaii	80.00
Shock Absorber	7.95
Motor Oil, qt.	.29
Tires, set of 4	79.95
Round Trip Train Fare Chicago to L.A.	125.84

HOME & HEARTH

Bath Towel	$ 3.98
Bedspread, full	9.98
Broom	.66
Electric Percolator	18.89
Garden Hose	.67
Hi-Fi w/3 Speakers	219.95
Iron	17.95
Ladder	7.10
Lawnmower	109.95
Paint, gal.	2.88
Radio	24.99
Refrigerator	198.88
Television, 24˝	359.95
Toaster, pop-up	10.88
Vacuum Cleaner	69.95
Washing Machine	164.80

SPANKING
NEW FULL-SIZE DODGE
PRICED MODEL FOR MODEL
WITH FORD AND
CHEVROLET

DART!!

The new automobile you are looking at is a 1961 Dodge called Dart!! It is upsetting automotive applecarts all over the place. Why? Because Dart is a full-size Dodge priced model-for-model with Ford and Chevrolet. It has Dodge room, Dodge comfort and Dodge quality throughout. It has a rust-proofed, rattle-proofed unitized body. It has a battery-saving alternator-generator. It rides beautifully. It is just about the most economical family-size car going. Dart has many good things, twenty-three models for instance. You'll like Dart!! See your Dodge Dealer. You'll like him, too.

WAGES

Weekly

Dance Teacher	$ 85
Hairdresser	100
Broadway Actor, minimum	103.50
Legal Secretary	110
Pharmacist	140
Jack Paar	4,100
Clark Gable, overtime for *"The Misfits"*	48,000

Yearly

Nurse	$ 4,380
Teacher	4,762
Bookkeeper	4,800
Lab Technician	5,000
Bank Teller	5,200
Executive Secretary	6,000
Art Director	8,000
General Practice Doctor	12,000
Congressperson	22,500

College Graduate Entry Level Monthly Wages

Journalist	$ 380
Advertising	400
Accountant	500
Engineer	600

ENTERTAINMENT

Playing Cards	$ .69
Museum of Modern Art Admission	.95
Silly Putty	1.00
Movie	1.00-3.50
Circus	1.50 adults .75 kids
Pete Seeger at Carnegie Hall	2.00 lowest price
YWCA Yearly Membership	2.50
LP Record	4.98
Broadway Play (*The Sound Of Music*)	9.90 top price

STOCKS

GENERAL MOTORS	41
GETTY OIL	16
GOODRICH	72 1/4
PEPSI COLA	38 3/4
POLAROID	186 1/2
RCA	70 1/2

1960 CAR CORNER

FORD MOTOR CO.

Ford introduces the **Comet** to compete with the Volkswagen and other compact cars.

- The one-millionth compact is produced by the U.S. auto industry.

- Six million cars are sold this year with 80% of U.S. families owning cars.

- Rack-and-pinion steering pioneered by TRW.

- Lincoln Continental extends its guarantee from three months or 4,000 miles to two years or 24,000 miles.

Studebaker-Packard offers $100 rebate to any of its 200,000 shareholders who purchase a 1960 Lark.

Nash Production *Discontinued By* American Motors.

Chrysler *Discontinues Its*
De Soto
Line After 32 Years.

PASSING

Philanthropist, humanitarian and heir to one of the world's biggest fortunes, **John D. Rockefeller, Jr.** dies at 86, leaving behind a legacy of generosity. He donated approximately $450 million to science, medicine, education, museums, parks and religion. His $150 million estate is divided between family and various charities.

WHAT A YEAR IT WAS!

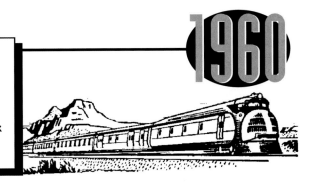

1960

In the largest such merger of the 20th century, the Interstate Commerce Commission approves merger of the Erie Railroad and the Delaware, Lackawanna & Western Railroad.

CROISSANTS & CURRENT EVENTS
The *New York Times* establishes a Paris edition.

PASSING THE MANTLE
60-year old publisher of the *Los Angeles Times*, **Norman Chandler**, announces his retirement with his son, **Otis**, assuming the leadership role.

CASH FLOW PROBLEM
Howard Hughes, one of the world's richest men, is short $340 million to pay for jet planes ordered for his TWA but backs out of deal requiring him to turn over control to three trustees.

- Japan Airlines to purchase its fifth $5 million DC-8 jetliner from Douglas Aircraft.

- Pan American Airways takes over 613,000 sq. ft. on 15 floors of the 59-story skyscraper to be built over Grand Central Terminal making it the biggest office space lease deal ever made in Manhattan.

- Pan American Airways opens the world's most beautiful terminal at New York's Idlewild International Airport spending a record $12 million on the glass-and-steel circular structure.

GOODBYE ROCKIN' DAYS AT THE ROXY

Manhattan real estate tycoon **William Zeckendorf** buys the Roxy Theatre from Rockefeller Center Inc. for $5,000,000 and plans to add on to his Taft Hotel which would make it one of the largest hotels in New York.

Insurance companies doing interstate business via mail are subject to regulations set down by the Federal Trade Commission according to a U.S. Supreme Court ruling.

BEST RUN COMPANIES IN THE U.S.

(A Dun's Review Survey of 171 Presidents)

E.I. du Pont

General Electric

General Motors

International Business Machines

Minnesota Mining & Manufacturing Co.

DON'T THROW STONES

In its new glass-and-concrete structure the nation's biggest bank, the **Bank Of America**, boasts the most highly automated commercial bank in the country.

DIAMONDS IN THE ROUGH

South Africa's De Beers announces that it has agreed to market Russian diamonds.

THE WALK-UP PHONE

Busy Americans are making more phone calls—and the Bell System is making service more convenient. This newest public telephone, the Walk-Up, saves time and steps for everybody. Your town will find it as handy as the corner mailbox.

THE DRIVE-UP PHONE

Like the drive-in movie and drive-in bank, this is a natural for a nation on wheels. Late for a party or appointment? Forget something at home or office? Need room reservations miles ahead? Just drive up to the Drive-Up and dial.

NEW PUBLIC PHONES
to serve you in new ways and places

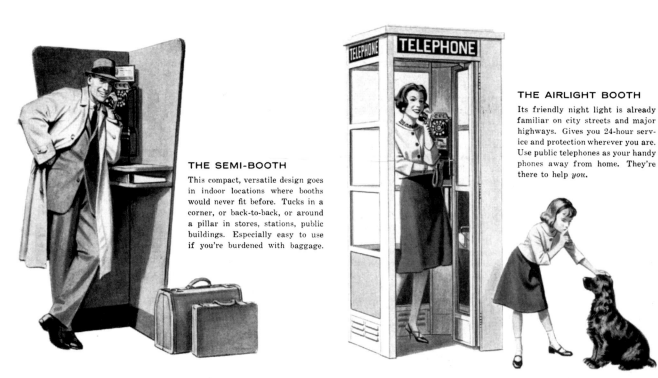

THE SEMI-BOOTH

This compact, versatile design goes in indoor locations where booths would never fit before. Tucks in a corner, or back-to-back, or around a pillar in stores, stations, public buildings. Especially easy to use if you're burdened with baggage.

THE AIRLIGHT BOOTH

Its friendly night light is already familiar on city streets and major highways. Gives you 24-hour service and protection wherever you are. Use public telephones as your handy phones away from home. They're there to help *you*.

BELL TELEPHONE SYSTEM

SCIENCE 1960

FROZEN STIFF

Perfectly preserved remains of two 2,600-year old seals discovered in Antarctica.

Hughes Aircraft scientist Dr. Theodore H. Maiman announces the development of a device called a *"Laser"* which creates an atomic radio-light brighter than the sun's center.

FOLLOWING THE BOUNCING RED BEAM

U.S. scientists Arthur Schawlow and Charles Townes develop maser device using microwaves.

Columbia University scientists discover an underwater island thought to be inhabited 8,000 to 10,000 years ago in the south Atlantic, west of the Cape of Good Hope, South Africa.

NOT BAD FOR A 5,400-YEAR OLD

The oldest mummified body in the world is discovered in the Libyan desert.

HEY BRO, WHAT'S HAPPENIN'

First human ancestor Homo habilis fossils estimated to be 1.6 to 1.9 million-years old discovered at Olduvai Gorge, Tanzania by a team led by anthropologists Mary and Louis Leakey.

Departing from Pearl Harbor, U.S. atomic submarine **Sargo** reaches the North Pole in 22 days.

WHERE'S MIKE TODD WHEN YOU NEED HIM?
U.S. nuclear submarine **Triton** completes its record underwater journey around the world in 84 days.

Two Polaris missiles fired for the first time from a submerged U.S. Navy submarine.

The first U.S. submarine armed with thermonuclear missiles — "**U.S.S. George Washington**" — sails from Charleston, South Carolina on its first patrol.

U.S. nuclear submarine "Seadragon" makes the first underwater navigation of the Northwest Passage.

The U.S. Navy launches the "Ethan Allen" — its most powerful atomic submarine.

⚓ The U.S. Navy bathyscape Trieste breaks existing dive record descending 24,000 feet in the Pacific Ocean off Guam.

⚓ U.S. Navy Lieutenant Don Walsh and record holder Jacques Piccard descend a record 35,800 feet in the bathyscape Trieste breaking its own previous record.

The largest warship ever built, first U.S. atomic-powered aircraft carrier, **U.S.S. Enterprise**, with capabilities of cruising around the world 20 times without refueling, is launched at Newport News, Virginia.

WHAT A YEAR IT WAS!

Mt. Palomar astronomer Dr. Rudolph Minkowski reports that he photographed the most distant object ever identified — a celestial object about six billion light-years away from earth.

SUN WATCH

Construction begins on the world's largest solar telescope to be installed in the Kitt Peak National Observatory located in a remote section of Arizona Indian country.

WHEN YOU WISH UPON AN AGING STAR

Cornell University astronomers believe the earth was born billions of years ago from the debris of exploding Red Giant stars some of which fell apart because of old age.

AND NOW FOR YOUR LISTENING PLEASURE

The Western World's largest radio telescope, capable of listening to radiation signals billions of light-years away, is under construction at Sugar Grove, West Virginia.

HEY HONEY THAT LOOKS LIKE A GOOD PARKING SPOT

In preparation to select lunar landing sites for manned and unmanned spacecraft, the U.S. Geological Survey completes the first known photogeological survey of the surface of the moon.

1960

DON'T UPSET HAL

The FATHER OF CYBERNETICS, Doctor Norbert Wiener, warns that thinking machines threaten to enslave their creators.

American scientist J.E. Steel coins the term BIONICS to describe creating devices and machines modeled on living organisms and their parts.

THERE'LL BE A HOT TIME IN THE OLD TOWN TONIGHT

Biggest nuclear plant in the U.S. and first commercially operated atomic energy reactor is dedicated in Dresden, Illinois by Commonwealth Edison.

☢ Controlled thermonuclear reaction lasting 1/1,000 of a second is accomplished at Lawrence Radiation Laboratory in Livermore, California.

☢ For the first time, the U.S. publishes pictures of atomic bombs of the type used on Japan in 1945.

☢ Dr. Roberts Rugh, Associate Professor at the radiological research laboratory of Columbia University, concludes that developing embryos are especially sensitive to radiation, the effects of which might not surface for generations.

Lockheed Missiles and Space Division demonstrate rocket engine that enables satellites to change orbit in space.

First stage of von Braun's Saturn rocket engine is tested.

A target 9,000 miles away in the Indian Ocean is the destination of the Atlas ICBM fired from Cape Canaveral.

Army announces first recorded interception of one guided missile by another.

Russians launch "Super Rockets" 8,000 miles into central Pacific.

EXACTLY HOW DID YOU SAY WE SHOULD WALK THE DOGS?

Soviet Union announces the launching, orbiting and safe return of **Sputnik V** - a second 5-ton satellite carrying two dogs, Strelka and Belka, as well as other animals and an assortment of insects and plant life.

The Seven "Project Mercury" Astronauts, Expected To Be America's Pioneer Space Travellers, Train At Lewis' Multiple Axis Space Test Inertia Facility To Learn How To Control Tumbling Spacecraft.

The Strategic Air Command Creates First Squadron Of The B-58 **Hustler** Capable Of Twice The Speed Of Sound For Short Distances With Nuclear Bombs Aboard.

A New Nonstop Record Is Set By A B-52 Bomber Flying 10,000 Miles Without Refueling.

UP, UP & AWAY IN MY BEAUTIFUL BALLOON

USAF Parachutist Captain Joseph Kittinger, Jr. sets new world record, free falling 16 miles at 450 m.p.h. from a balloon, opening his parachute at 17,500 ft. taking 13 minutes, 8 seconds to complete the leap.

LANDING IN A FOGGY DAY IN LONDON TOWN

British European Airways Airliner Tests First Completely Automatic Landing System — Autoland — Designed By Britain's Royal Aircraft Establishment.

America's Newest Air Traffic Control System Goes Into Operation At San Francisco International Airport Providing Instant Communication Between All Controllers.

BALLISTIC MISSILE EARLY WARNING SYSTEM

• The Free World's First Missile-Detecting Radar Station Designed To Warn North America Of Long-Range Ballistic Missile Attacks Becomes Operational At Thule, Greenland.

• An Early Warning Long-Range Radar Station In Yorkshire, England To Be Established Jointly By The U.S. And Great Britain.

WHAT A YEAR IT WAS!

NEITHER RAIN NOR SHINE NOR HAIL NOR SLEET ESCAPES THIS CAMERA

Tiros I, The First U.S. Satellite Designed Specifically To Send Back Detailed TV Photos Of The Earth's Weather Patterns, Is Launched From Cape Canaveral And In Three Months Sends Back 25,000 Pictures Of The Weather From Over 400 Miles Up.

ONE IF BY LAND — TWO IF BY SEA — THREE IF BY OUTER SPACE

The U.S. Navy Launches Experimental "Space Lighthouse" **Transit IB** Designed To Assist In Navigation.

• U.S. Planetoid **Pioneer V** Is Launched Into Orbit Around The Sun From Cape Canaveral, Florida.

• **Pioneer V** Signals Emanating From 409,000 Miles In Space Are Received At U.S. Tracking Stations Two Days After Launch.

• The U.S. Air Force Launches **Midas II**, A 5,000 Lb. Satellite Programmed To Warn Against Surprise Missile Attacks.

• U.S. Air Force Succeeds In Recovering In Midair A 300 Lb. Instrument Capsule Ejected From Satellite **Discovery XIV**.

• Manned Space Test Station Predicted By 1970 For Scientific Research Of Space.

• The 100 Ft. In Diameter U.S. Balloon Communications Satellite **Echo I** Goes Into Orbit.

• U.S. Launches **Courier IB** — First Active Telecommunications Satellite.

NOBEL PRIZES

MEDICINE & PHYSIOLOGY	PHYSICS	CHEMISTRY
The prize was awarded jointly to **Sir F. MacFarlane Burnet** (Australia) and **Sir Peter B. Medawar** (Great Britain)	**Donald A. Glaser** (U.S.A.)	**Willard F. Libby** (U.S.A.)

QUALITY NEW COMER FROM PONTIAC!

TEMPEST

AMERICA'S ONLY FRONT ENGINE ⟺ REAR TRANSMISSION CAR

155 H.P. FROM FOUR CYLINDERS!*

PRICED WITH THE COMPACTS!

*WITH 4-BARREL CARBURETOR AND AUTOMATIC TRANSMISSION, EXTRA-COST OPTIONS

LOOK MA, NO TEETH

A study conducted by the Commission on the Survey of Dentistry reveals among other things that Americans set a low priority on dental care and that there is a shortage of dentists with a ratio of one dentist to 1,697 people.

LOOK INTO MY EYES

A study of over 400 dental patients at the University of Melbourne reveals that eye color seems to determine the amount of pain a patient can tolerate with dark-eyed patients suffering the most and blue-eyed patients suffering the least.

SEE YOU AT THE WATER COOLER

Coffee breaks are considered a healthy, stress-reducing activity where co-workers can visit with each other creating an opportunity to share experiences and let off steam.

NOSING AROUND FOR THE TRUTH

The sense of smell is sharpest when the lining of the nose is red, wet and slightly swollen says a study done at the University of Oklahoma Medical School.

Drivers of the new smaller cars are developing pains in the chest, hip or back areas a day or two after they begin driving these cars.

THE CREEPY CRAWLIES

Even the most-scrubbed among us are covered with approximately ten trillion germs spread out over 19 square feet of skin but fortunately most of them are harmless.

GOING TO THE DOGS

Research out of the College of Veterinary Medicine at Michigan State University indicates that sick cats recover faster when placed in the same ward as dogs.

CUDDLE UP A LITTLE CLOSER

When deprived of their soft cuddly mother, monkeys get sick and even die leading researchers at the University Of Wisconsin to conclude that cuddling of babies is just as important as feeding for their well-being.

LET'S CHILL OUT

Los Angeles physician Dr. Alex Shulman recommends ice water therapy to relieve the pain from burns.

DOCTOR, HEAL THYSELF

2,000 Physicians In The U.S. Are Or Will Be Addicted To Narcotics Says *Medico-legal Digest*.

General practitioners experience more heart attacks than any other group of physicians.

A new method for reviving the heart without opening the chest is developed at Johns Hopkins University by applying pressure with one hand on the top of the other downward on the patient's breast bone about 60 times a minute.

New artificial kidney successfully used on patients with kidney failure.

The Arthritis and Rheumatism Foundation reports that Americans spend over $250 million a year on quack remedies.

American College of Surgeons point out that an excessive amount of antibiotics are being given to patients in hospitals resulting in unnecessary medical costs.

Researchers at Madison State Hospital in Madison, Indiana report that mixing alcohol with tranquilizers such as Miltown produces a more intoxicated state than alcohol alone.

New York specialist assures women that hair loss is probably temporary and could be caused by hard brushes, setting lotions, a too-tight hairdo, poor nutrition or disease.

According to Dr. Jerome M. Kummer of the University of California Medical School at Los Angeles one out of five pregnancies in the U.S. is terminated through criminal abortion.

SPEAK SOFTLY AND FORGET THE STICK

One way of living longer, according to Chicago's Dr. Morris Fishbein, is by not raising your voice and speaking in a calm tone thereby avoiding stress which is one of the principal causes of aging.

WHAT DO YOU MEAN YOU FEEL GREAT?

A study conducted at Tulane University over a 12-year period on 10,709 people indicates that 9 out of 10 have a disease or abnormality without showing any symptoms.

THE SELF-MADE MAN—WHAT PRICE SUCCESS?

Young business executives who begin climbing the career ladder immediately on graduating high school experience more illnesses than their college graduate counterparts, tending to be overweight smokers who marry at a younger age and experience more financial worries.

JUST HOW OLD ARE YOU, OLD PAL?

Men lie about their age more often than women concludes a survey printed in the *Journal Of The American Geriatrics Society* with the most lying done by the 30 to 50-year old group.

HEY BECKY WHY DON'T YOU START WITHOUT ME AND I'LL JOIN YOU AS SOON AS I WALK TO THE BED

A study reveals that healthy old people continue to have sex beyond the age of 90.

STAYING YOUNG IN MIND, SPIRIT AND BODY
(7 Rules Recommended By The AMA)

✓ **Regular medical check-ups**

✓ **Eat healthfully and stay trim**

✓ **Get plenty of rest for your mind and body**

✓ **Exercise**

✓ **Be productive with your time**

✓ **Participate in community affairs**

✓ **Prepare for your future financial needs**

Dr. Kenneth L. McCoy *Of Providence Hospital In Washington, D.C. Develops A Vaccine Against Staphylococci.*

Aspirin **Found To Help** *Lower Blood Sugar In Diabetics.*

The 300-Year Old Tuberculosis Epidemic *Is Officially Coming To An End In Europe.*

Dr. D.C. Stuart, Jr. *of the New York Department of Health Laboratories isolates and photographs for the first time the polio virus inside the human cell in which they are formed discovering that the viruses are formed in the cytoplasm surrounding the nucleus and not in the nucleus itself as had been the belief.*

The Sabin Oral Vaccine *Made Of Live Poliomyelitis Viruses Receives Approval For Use In The United States By The Surgeon General.*

The Merck Institute for Therapeutic Research *Develops A More Potent Salk Polio Vaccine Raising Protection Level To 91%.*

HOSPITAL CARE OF THE FUTURE —
A PREDICTION

➕ Upon checking into the radioactive fallout-resistant underground hospital through above-ground towers with elevator access to floors below, the patient will be anesthetized and kept unconscious until discharged;

➕ Patient will be attached to electrical devices that will monitor pain, pulse, respiration, skin color, brain waves, evaporation and heart activity;

➕ Feeding will be intravenous or through a stomach tube;

➕ Patients with infections will be isolated in an antiseptic building and treated without human hands.

➕ The anesthetized patient will receive treatments at 10 to 12 treatment centers which he will be sent to through a series of pneumatic tubes.

➕ An IBM machine will diagnose the ailment, prescribe and commence treatment after analyzing data received from an electronic scanner used on the patient.

PASSINGS

Dr. Ernest Goodpasture, who created a method for mass-developing vaccines against smallpox, influenza, yellow fever and typhus, dies at age 73.

HEY MAN, I HEAR MICKEY MOUSE IS RUNNING FOR OFFICE — COOL!

In Her Book *What College Students Think* Professor Rose K. Goldsen Concludes That Today's Students Are Politically Disinterested, Apathetic And Conservative.

Chicago Doctors Find Head-Banging Infants Usually Have A Highly-Developed Sense Of Rhythm.

A Harvard Medical School doctor discourages parents from punishing their children for bed-wetting indicating that it is simply a matter of the bladder being too small to hold the urine all those hours and that by the time the child is 4 1/2 the bladder capacity should double from age 2.

WHAT'S SO HAPPY ABOUT CHILDHOOD?

Conflict is a major activity of preschool children with one occurring every five minutes for youngsters from two to four years of age.

HEALTH FUTURES GOING UP IN SMOKE

Although two out of three teenagers see a connection between smoking and lung cancer, 21% or one in five in junior and senior high schools are smoking with boys representing 13%.

GO ASK YOUR FATHER

Research reveals that parents who act as a unit tend to be stricter with their children than when they act individually.

COME ON KIDS, LET'S HIT THOSE JUNGLE JIMS

One out of four children in the U.S. is obese.

According to a 17-year study of burn cases admitted to Children's Orthopedic Hospital in Seattle, Washington, spilled coffee or tea is the most common cause of burns to children.

TIME OUT FOR LEFTY

Dr. Godfrey E. Arnold, clinical director of the National Hospital for Speech Disorders in New York, contends that it is basically unnatural to use the left hand in a right-handed world and that switching a child's left-hand preference is not harmful.

The blood cholesterol role

in heart attacks is one of the most debated issues in medicine with a growing number of researchers committed to the idea that foods high in this fat-like substance such as cream, cheese, butter, ice cream, fatty meats, bacon and lard should be eliminated and there should be greater use of corn, cottonseed or soya oils. Other key factors are elevation in blood pressure and family history.

In researching the reasons Italians have a lower rate of coronary disease than Americans, Minneapolis physiologist Ancel Keys discovers a key ingredient in the Italian diet is pectin and that taking 15 grams daily for three weeks lowered blood cholesterol levels. Two apples daily provide proper pectin.

TWO APPLES A DAY KEEPS THE CHOLESTEROL AWAY

PUMP THOSE IRONS

In order to enjoy good health and longevity, exercise is strongly urged to maintain a tonic state of the body.

SOMETHING TO KEEP THE OLD TICKER TICKING

Surgeons in Birmingham develop a pacemaker for the heart.

TIME TO SLOW DOWN BUDDY

Excessive adrenaline present in competitive, hard-driving men seems to be a direct link to heart disease.

PUT THIS "B" IN YOUR BONNET

A Soviet nutritionist recommends extra B-Complex vitamins to combat nervous and mental stress.

the battle of the bulge, continued

Medical evidence analyzed by the Food and Drug Administration fails to support claims that electric vibrating machines melt away fat.

Blaming eating fads and dieting for the death of hundreds and the illness of thousands yearly, famous anthropologist **Dr. Margaret Mead** says that Americans are not well nourished due to high-caloric, low-nutrition foods.

good news for noshers

According to **Dr. Clarence Cohn** of Chicago's Michael Reese Hospital based on his chicken experiments, three big meals a day could be injurious to your heart and the same amount of food should be broken up into smaller, more frequent meals.

a growing nation

With 55% of American adults being overweight or obese, hospitalization is recommended for obese people who can't stick to a diet so their "cheating" can be curtailed.

The AMA releases report indicating there is no drug that will melt excess fat.

PSYCHIATRY

GET OFF THE DIME

An Air Force Office of Scientific Research funded study on decision making conducted by psychologists at Ohio State University concludes that executives who tend to procrastinate in making decisions are more apt to make the wrong decision than those executives who make decisions quickly.

I THINK I JUST CAUGHT A CASE OF PARANOIA

According to Dr. Richard J. Plunkett, director of the American Medical Association's Mental Health Department, while mental illness is not a germ that can be transmitted, some mental disturbances can be projected onto another person.

LAUGHING MATTERS

A 10-year study conducted at Yale University on the role of humor and laughter reveals that mentally ill people generally do not have a sense of humor and that the pursuit of laughter and humor is vital to one's well being with a bad joke being better than no joke at all.

BRITISH DOCTOR GIVES WIVES TIPS ON NOT KILLING THEIR HUSBANDS

- Don't insist on having the last word;
- Be cheerful when he comes home from work;
- Humor him;
- Don't tell him he's wrong all the time;
- Make your home a safe haven from the busy world.

Experiments in isolation conducted on normal people reveal that deprived of their usual ways of dealing with various stimuli such as light and sound they begin to display neurotic behavior as soon as three hours after the isolation begins.

Fainting can sometimes be a psychosomatic reaction to an unpleasant situation.

Americans have developed a new phobia called radiophobia which is fear of radiation or "nuclear neurosis."

PAGING DR. LEARY, PAGING DR. LEARY

Two Beverly Hills doctors report using LSD as a facilitating agent in treating patients at their Psychiatric Institute of Beverly Hills, expanding a regular psychotherapy session from the traditional 50 minutes to up to five or six hours.

New PRODUCTS And INVENTIONS

PILLSBURY introduces refrigerated chocolate chip cookies which are sliced into chunks and then baked.

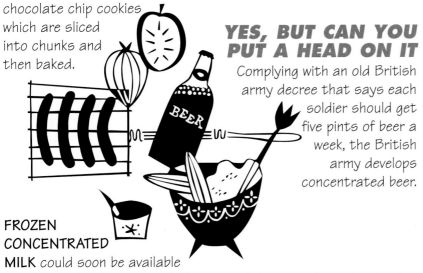

YES, BUT CAN YOU PUT A HEAD ON IT

Complying with an old British army decree that says each soldier should get five pints of beer a week, the British army develops concentrated beer.

FROZEN CONCENTRATED MILK could soon be available thanks to the University of Wisconsin dairy scientists who develop a freezing method.

HOW PINK IT IS

U.S. Department of Agriculture scientists develop naturally colored pink grapefruit juice.

SOME LIKE IT TO STAY HOT

Your pizza will now be hot when it's delivered through the **Pizza Porter**, a special insulated zippered vinyl carrying case invented by Pizza Porter, Inc., of Syracuse, New York.

A REAL TURN-ON

Westinghouse offers housewives the opportunity of starting dinner before they get home by using the **Dial-an-Appliance**, a gadget that can turn on the oven by simply dialing a few digits.

YOU NO LONGER HAVE TO TREAD LIGHTLY

Italian manufacturer Pirelli Limited develops a tire with replaceable tread.

SOMETHING TO BOUNCE UP & DOWN ABOUT

R.M. Pierson of the Goodyear Tire & Rubber Company has developed a rubber valve that eventually can be used to replace diseased parts of a human heart.

Genie model 410 is introduced to operate oversize garage doors.

NO LONGER A DRAINING EXPERIENCE

In development for 25 years, E.I. du Pont de Nemours brings out a permanent antifreeze which never requires draining from the car's cooling system.

Car whose battery is recharged by solar cells is unveiled in N.Y.

YOUR TIME IS HIS TIME

Mario Baccara of Caracas, Venezuela invents a global clock that tells the correct time, date, hours of daylight and darkness and the time of sunrises and sunsets any place in the world.

WHAT A YEAR IT WAS!

PASSING

Co-creator early in the century of the disc clutch for automobiles, **George W. Borg** dies at age 72.

TV

Sony introduces the world's first transistor television.

Motorola introduces a totally transistorized 19" big screen television receiver.

As If One Dimension Isn't Bad Enough

Westinghouse Electric exhibits an experimental 3-D television set at the Chicago Home Furnishings Show.

For transmitting handwritten, typed or printed copy a public facsimile service called Wirefax is established between Chicago, Los Angeles, New York City, San Francisco and Washington D.C.

A Telex service is established between Great Britain and the U.S.

PHONES OF THE FUTURE

Bell Telephone is testing a new phone in Morris, Illinois with the following experimental capabilities:

- Dial two digits instead of seven to reach frequently called numbers.
- If the first line is busy, incoming calls are automatically routed to another phone.
- Forward calls to another telephone number.
- Extension phones can be converted into intercom units by dialing two digits.

HELLO? Is This The Person I've Been Trying To Get Through To For The Last Hour?

Southwestern Bell Telephone is ready to install telephone equipment with a built-in memory which will automatically redial a number that has been busy.

WHEN YOU SPEAK, THEY MAY NOT BE LISTENING

New York's Mosler Research Products, Inc. develops a phone line they claim is "tap proof."

Let The Cell Phone Games Begin

The Federal Communications Commission grants AT&T authority to establish public air to ground operations for airborne radio-telephone service on a limited number of radio bands.

El Al Israel Airlines announces on-board telephone service along its international routes for a cost of $3.00-$9.00 a minute.

Bell Telephone System develops an electronic hand-held device which creates a voice when placed against the throat, allowing people whose larynx has been paralyzed or removed to speak.

Bulova Watch Co. Develops World's First Electronic Wrist Watch.

IS THAT A RECORD PLAYER IN YOUR POCKET OR ARE YOU JUST HAPPY TO SEE ME?

Emerson brings the **Wondergram** to the marketplace — a pocket-size portable record player.

FATHER OF THE LONG-PLAYING DISC DOES IT AGAIN

The Zenith Radio Corporation is scheduled to manufacture long-play tape machines perfected by Dr. Peter Goldmark at Columbia Broadcasting System Laboratories.

WHO NEEDS A BACK-UP BAND

Wurlitzer Co. of De Kalb, Illinois develops **Side Man**, an electronic rhythm instrument that provides background at different tempos for musical instruments offering a variety of sounds including drums, cymbals, tom-toms and an assortment of rhythms and beats from cha cha to waltz to fox trot.

HEARING IS BELIEVING

Sonotone Corp. of Elmsford, New York is marketing a hearing aid the size of a lump of sugar weighing only half an ounce.

BIG BROTHER IS WATCHING YOU

Denver, Colorado tests a traffic camera that serves as a traffic counter as well as regulating the timing of stoplights.

SMILE, Your Deposit's On Camera

A bank night deposit machine with separate compartments for coins and checks is developed providing the depositor with a photograph-receipt of his deposits.

SMILE, You're On Camera

Closed-circuit television camera installed in elevator of a New York luxury apartment to monitor and protect tenants.

MAJOR TOM TO GROUND CONTROL

A new helmet designed to transmit messages to earth by picking up vibrations of an astronaut's voice through his skull bones is being developed at the School of Aviation Medicine in San Antonio, Texas.

TAKE TWO ASPIRINS AND CALL ME IN 300 LIGHT-YEARS

The first graduates of space medicine studies at the Air Force School of Aviation Medicine at Brooks Air Force Base receive space diplomas.

YOU WON'T SEE ITS DUST

General Electric Company Creates Vacu-Magic — a vacuum cleaner for phonograph records.

A SALTY SUBJECT

Purported to be 100 times more effective than previous commercial membranes, researchers at University of California, Los Angeles develop a membrane to filter salt out of sea water.

REDOING THOSE CART-WHEELS

If you're thinking of making off with that shopping cart, Detroit's Super Market Controls, Inc. has developed magnetic brakes that lock the wheels of the cart if you try wheeling it out of the store's parking lot.

If you want to be protected against nuclear radiation hazards and radioactive fallout, carry *FIDO*, a pocket-size alarm which gets louder as radiation intensity increases.

AND FOR THOSE OF YOU STILL IN THE DARK

Protect-O-Lite is a photoelectric eye light control switch activated by the presence or absence of light which turns on lights at night and off at dawn.

WESTERN UNION NEWS

• The world's largest private high-speed communications network linking air bases around the world is put into operation by Western Union for the U.S. Air Force.

• Western Union begins construction of a transcontinental microwavebeam network designed to handle all forms of electronic communication including high-speed transmission of data, alternate record-voice facsimile, telegraph, digitalized TV and other communication services.

• A nationwide bomb alarm system designed to alert the nation's military and civilian leaders within one second of a nuclear blast at any strategic U.S. location is installed by Western Union.

CATCHING BABY'S FIRST BURPS

Fairchild Camera has introduced the world's first 8-millimeter home movie camera with sound for $239.50.

PLEASE DON'T TELL TED TURNER

Technicolor Corp. of Hollywood develops technology that allows making color motion picture film from a black and white original.

AN END TO LONG FLIGHT BOREDOM

Inflight Motion Pictures, Inc. of New York City develops a motion picture projection system allowing airlines to show movies to their passengers for the first time.

8mm Fairchild Cinephonic with 13mm f/1.8 Cinphar lens, $249

Why does this revolutionary 8mm movie camera have a mike? The best reason's at the end of the cord.

Until a few short months ago, all home movies were *silent*. Then along came the Fairchild Cinephonic.

Except for the mike, it looks like any other 8mm camera. It handles like any other, too. But as you film the action, the Cinephonic records the sound *automatically*.

Where once a locomotive whistled unheard, or a five-year-old scalping party whooped in silence, *now there is sound*. Where laughter, voices once were lost, *now they're on film*. Impossible six months ago. Simple today.

The Cinephonic is incredibly easy to operate. You wear the microphone around your neck—or hide it in the scene. You move as freely, shoot as freely as ever, indoors or out. The entire recording mechanism is *inside* the camera. Yet the camera weighs a scant five pounds, loaded.

Cinephonic *film*—in color or black-and-white—is the equal of the finest film you have ever used. It is edged with a narrow magnetic recording stripe. Sound is permanently synchronized with action.

Hearing is believing! Better camera stores and camera departments gladly demonstrate. They report snowballing interest in the Cinephonic. It seems everyone wants to know more about the camera-with-a-mike.

* * *

The Cinephonic projector—as new as the camera—shows your new sound movies, adds sound to your silent films as well. $259.

FAIRCHILD CINEPHONIC®

A PRODUCT OF FAIRCHILD CAMERA AND INSTRUMENT CORPORATION © 1960

The famous cold-water soap, *Woolite*, is now available in liquid form and comes packaged in a plastic container.

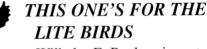

KEEPING IT ZIPPED
The Talon Company introduces the **Plastic Coil Zipper**.

Dr. Timothy Takaro, Chief of the Cardiovascular Section of the Oteen, North Carolina VA Hospital, invents a new stapling device enabling a surgeon to join blood vessels together rapidly.

LOOK MA, NO CAVITIES
For cavity reduction, the American Dental Association endorses a commercial product for the first time — **Crest Toothpaste**.

NO MORE SLIP-SLIDING AWAY
You can slip-proof your bathtub with **Don't Slip**, adhesive strips that adhere to the bottom of the tub.

Removing Toe Jammin' Blues
The Woodworth Toe Cleaner Co. of Binghamton, New York offers a new brush designed to massage and clean under and around the toes.

ARE YOU LISTENING MR. NIXON?
Remington Rand introduces an electric shaver that shaves for up to three weeks before requiring recharging.

CANNING THE CAN OPENERS
Alcoa Aluminum is testing a new orange juice can with a tabbed top.

IT'S A DOG'S LIFE
Prefabricated doghouses sold in supermarkets for $15.95.

THIS ONE'S FOR THE LITE BIRDS
Wilhelm E. Poulsen invents a bird-feeder designed to feed little birds only through use of a weight-sensitive perch which dips and closes the door when one of the bigger birds drop in for a bite.

NEW TOYS FOR TOTS		
Chatty Cathy	(Mattel)	$18.00
Mr. Machine	(Ideal)	12.00
The Fighting Lady	(Remco)	12.98
A Giant Bulldozer	(Louis Marx)	15.00

CORRECTING THE ERRORS OF YOUR WAYS
TYPE-OUT, a chemically treated paper that is placed over a typo, removes the error by retyping the same letter leaving a clean space for the correct letter.

THE KEY OF CLEAN
A typewriter cleaner that rolls into a typewriter like a sheet of paper and cleans the keys when it is typed on is introduced by Minnesota Mining & Manufacturing.

NO MORE FINGER INKING GOOD
PERMA-STAMP, a plastic device containing its own ink supply, does away with the stamp pad and allows 30,000 impressions without re-inking.

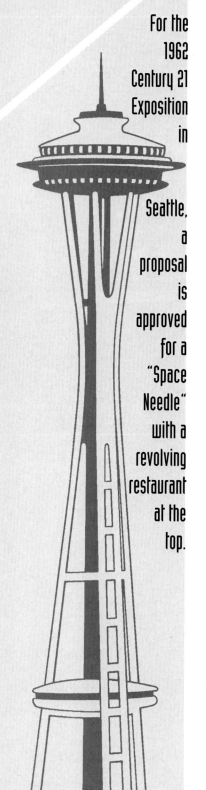

For the 1962 Century 21 Exposition in Seattle, a proposal is approved for a "Space Needle" with a revolving restaurant at the top.

EERO SAARINEN:

— Causes controversy when his modern U.S. Embassy opens in London.

— Becomes a fellow at the American Academy of Arts and Letters.

— Is hired by CBS to design their new quarters on 6th Avenue in midtown Manhattan.

In West Los Angeles work begins on Century City, a luxury shopping center that will include a Broadway department store and plentiful parking. The site is bought from 20th Century Fox Studios.

Plans are announced to develop Irvine Ranch, a 93,000-acre property near Los Angeles. Architect William Pereira envisions a self-contained community with houses, shops and a new branch of the University of California.

The newest and tallest building to begin construction on the M.I.T. campus is a creation of alumnus I.M. Pei.

NEW YORK, NEW YORK, WHAT A WONDERFUL TOWN

Because of the city's increasing importance in international business, the creation of a world trade center is discussed.

• **The National Design Center** devises a method for allowing women to view home furnishings samples before mass production begins, incorporating their suggestions into the final products.

• **Plans are announced** for a $100 million Grand Central City designed by **Walter Gropius** and **Pietro Belluschi**.

• **Ludwig Mies Van Der Rohe** receives the American Institute of Architects' Gold Medal.

• **A monastery opens in Eveux, France.** Created by **Le Corbusier**, the concrete and glass structure is linear, with pyramids and cubes scattered throughout.

• **Jean Cocteau** designs the inside of a church near Paris.

1960

Walnut remains the #1 wood choice in furniture, velvets and damasks are popular materials and bright colors — periwinkle, tangerine, purple, citron — are used sparingly in the home.

Affordable wood wallpaper called Microwood, coated with a thin veneer of various real woods, is now available.

After a long battle with the city of San Francisco over building codes, architect William Tabler is granted permission by a District Court to obtain the proper permit to begin erecting the much-anticipated $25 million San Francisco Hilton. Across the bay in Oakland, Welton Becket's $37 million Kaiser Center (below) opens.

A Michigan firm is marketing a prefabricated three bedroom house delivered to your lot in move-in condition for approximately $12,000.

Meanwhile, the Jim Walter Corp. sells unfinished homes from $1,395 for the handy types capable of installing their own finishing touches, such as plumbing and heating.

Ray and **Charles Eames** are awarded the first Kaufmann International Design Award.

Sure sign of
new home quality –
Briggs Beautyware
plumbing fixtures

Modern today and for years to come—that's Briggs Beautyware in your home. The exclusive Briggs design has won the acclaim of leading architects for its timeless grace and sweep of line, its clean, functional styling.

Briggs Beautyware enhances any home, enhances any decor. It is available in six decorator-styled colors that are fused right in. The result: true colors that resist acids and fading. In addition, Briggs bathtubs have slip-resistant bottoms, to be sure.

When looking for your new home, look for Briggs Beautyware. It is your sure sign of builder quality. Briggs Manufacturing Company, Warren, Michigan.

BRIGGS
B E A U T Y W A R E

94

music...

Blowin' Into New York

22-year old folk singer/composer **Bob Dylan** arrives in New York to sing in Greenwich Village night spots.

movies...

Preminger Helps Put An End To The Pain & Suffering

Defying the blacklisting of the Hollywood Ten, **Otto Preminger** hires Oscar-winning screenwriter **Dalton Trumbo** to write the screen version of **Leon Uris**' best seller *Exodus*.

Preminger

With the opening almost a year away, **Otto Preminger's** *Exodus* sets an all-time advance sale record.

TAKING A SHOWER WILL NEVER BE THE SAME AGAIN

Alfred Hitchcock shoots *Psycho* in just over a month.

PSYCHO **BREAKS ALL BOX OFFICE RECORDS.**

theatre...

PULITZER PRIZE FOR DRAMA

Fiorello!

Tom Bosley (right) and Nathaniel Frey

WHAT'S PLAYING AT THE MOVIES

The Bellboy
Bells Are Ringing
The Big Night
Butterfield 8
Can-Can
Cimarron
Cinderfella
Comanche Station
Crack In The Mirror
The Dark At The Top Of The Stairs
ELMER GANTRY
The Entertainer
EXODUS
Five Branded Women
From The Terrace
THE FUGITIVE KIND
G.I. BLUES
The Grass Is Greener
The Great Imposter
Heller In Pink Tights
The House Of Usher
Inherit The Wind
It Takes A Thief
L'Avventura
Lies My Father Told Me
THE LITTLE SHOP OF HORRORS
The Lost World
The Magnificent Seven

THE ALAMO
All The Fine Young Cannibals
All The Young Men
The Angel Wore Red
The Apartment
The Battle Of The Sexes

Make Mine Mink
The Marriage-Go-Round
Midnight Lace
The Millionairess
Murder, Inc.
Never On Sunday
Ocean's 11
Once More, With Feeling
Our Man In Havana
Please Don't Eat The Daisies
PSYCHO
THE RAT RACE
Saturday Night And Sunday Morning
Seven Thieves
THE SIGN OF ZORRO
Sink The Bismarck!
Sons And Lovers
SPARTACUS
Strangers When We Meet
Studs Lonigan
The Sundowners
Sunrise At Campobello
Tarzan The Magnificent
The Tempest
THE TIME MACHINE
Tunes Of Glory
The Unforgiven
Village Of The Damned
The Virgin Spring

Visit To A Small Planet
The Wackiest Ship In The Army
Where The Boys Are
Who Was That Lady?
Wild River
The World Of Suzie Wong
Your Money Or Your Wife

1960

Academy Awards Ceremony

Janet Leigh and Tony Curtis name the nominees and winner of the award for best story and screenplay.

And the winners for story are Russell Rouse and Clarence Greene with screenplay by Sammy Stanley and Maurice Richlin for *Pillow Talk*.

Susan Hayward presents Best Actor award to Charlton Heston for his performance in *Ben-Hur*.

Simone Signoret gets a big kiss from Rock Hudson as he presents her the Oscar for Best Actress for her performance in *Room At The Top*.

METRO GOLDWYN MAYER
WILLIAM WYLER'S
BEN-HUR

BEST PICTURE
BEN-HUR

BEST ACTOR
Charlton Heston : *Ben-Hur*

BEST ACTRESS
Simone Signoret : *Room At The Top*

BEST DIRECTOR
William Wyler : *Ben-Hur*

BEST SUPPORTING ACTOR
Hugh Griffith : *Ben-Hur*

BEST SUPPORTING ACTRESS
Shelley Winters : *The Diary Of Anne Frank*

BEST SONG
"High Hopes" : *A Hole In The Head*

1960 Favorites (Oscars Presented In 1961)

BEST PICTURE
The Apartment

BEST ACTOR
Burt Lancaster : *Elmer Gantry*

BEST ACTRESS
Elizabeth Taylor : *Butterfield 8*

BEST DIRECTOR
Billy Wilder : *The Apartment*

BEST SUPPORTING ACTOR
Peter Ustinov : *Spartacus*

BEST SUPPORTING ACTRESS
Shirley Jones : *Elmer Gantry*

BEST SONG
"Never On Sunday" : *Never On Sunday*

WHAT A YEAR IT WAS!

1960
the Academy Awards for 1960
For 1959 Films

"And The Winner Is..."

99

1960

GOLDEN GLOBE WORLD FILM FAVORITES:
- Rock Hudson
- Tony Curtis
- Gina Lollobrigida

CANNES FILM FESTIVAL PALM D'OR AWARD:
La Dolce Vita
Federico Fellini

METRO GOLDWYN MAYER
WILLIAM WYLER'S
BEN-HUR
Ben-Hur receives a record ten Oscars.

WHERE THERE'S JOKES — THERE'S HOPE
Bob Hope chosen to emcee the 32nd annual Academy Awards for the 8th time.

The Academy Awards Ceremony Moves To The Santa Monica Civic Auditorium.

Bob Hope and Bing Crosby to make another road film – **The Road To Hong Kong**.

PUTSKI UPSKI YOURSKI HANDSKI ANDSKI GIVESKI MESKI YOURSKI GOLDSKI
The Sword And The Dragon, the story of a Russian Robin Hood, is the first Soviet movie to be dubbed into English for American distribution.

The Apartment is the only American entry in the **Venice Film Festival**.

There's Something Fishy In Chicago
Mike Todd, Jr.'s **Smell-o-Vision** film *Scent Of Mystery* falls flat on its nose at its premiere.

Meanwhile In Outer Space...
MGM Buys Rights to Ray Bradbury's **The Martian Chronicles** for $150,000.

Walt Disney signs Kurt Russell to 10-year contract.

WE DON'T BLAME YOU JOANNE, WE'D STAY HOME, TOO
Oscar-winning actress Joanne Woodward says she may gradually retire from acting as she does not want to be separated from her husband, Paul Newman.

THESE STARS ARE MADE FOR WALKIN'
Official groundbreaking ceremonies are conducted for Hollywood's Walk Of Fame – actress Joanne Woodward gets first star on the Walk.

35% of films released this year are shot abroad.

Independent filmmakers are responsible for more than half the movies shot this year.

After a 17-year absence from the screen, 53-year old film actress **Anna May Wong** announces she's coming out of retirement.

Peter Lawford purchases the rights to *All In A Day* which he plans to produce and star in.

Lucille Ball suffers an injury during a filming session at Desilu Studios.

SPLENDOR IN THE BIG CITY

Natalie Wood and her husband **Bob Wagner** take up residency in New York while she films *Splendor In The Grass*.

WASN'T EXACTLY A BONDING EXPERIENCE

Hollywood stars **Dean Martin** and **Tony Martin** seek $100,000 from a Boston securities dealer accused of failing to complete a bond transaction they requested.

PLEASE, WHATEVER YOU DO, DON'T SMILE FOR THE CAMERA

Polynesian beauties are being interviewed to play Tahitian girls in the remake of *Mutiny On The Bounty* starring Marlon Brando on account of the Tahitian girls having bad teeth.

One of the Hollywood stars who pleaded for clemency for Caryl Chessman, **Marlon Brando** plans to produce and star in a film based on the famous convict's life.

WANT A LOLLYPOP LITTLE GIRL?

After an exhaustive search, director Stanley Kubrick finds his *Lolita* – **Sue Lyon** from Davenport, Iowa.

SOME LIKE HOT MONEY IN THE BANK

With Marilyn Monroe's reputation for being notoriously late preceding her, co-star of *The Misfits*, Clark Gable, stipulates in his contract that he will be guaranteed a 9-5 workday with a bonus of $48,000 a week if shooting goes past schedule.

While attending a party, college student **Peter Fonda** meets **Warren Beatty** for the first time and Beatty encourages him to pursue an acting career.

Henry Fonda's daughter **Jane** makes her screen debut in *Tall Story*.

Among the many notables attending this $12,000,000 hit in the film colony are Mary Livingston (*left*), Jack Benny and George Burns (*above*).

HOLLYWOOD

inda Christian and Yale
exler (*left*) wave to the
thusiastic fans lined up
catch a glimpse of their
vorite stars (*below*).

Tuesday Weld is
escorted by John Saxon
(*left*) and Dorothy
Malone shows up with
Jacques Bergerac
(*bottom*).

hails *SPARTACUS*

Cary Grant, arriving solo,
is dashing as ever.

Photographers pop their bulbs at the three
stars – John Gavin (left) Jean Simmons and
Kirk Douglas who plays the title role in this
spectacular drama of the gladiators' revolt.

WHAT A YEAR IT WAS!

1960 A RUSSIAN EXPORT

THE SOVIET FILM VERSION OF OTHELLO OPENS IN NEW YORK

Considered to be a high spot in the Soviet-American cultural exchange program the stars turn out to share in the celebration including Britain's lovely Sabrina (*above*) and escort, Lauren Bacall and Roddy McDowell (*right center*) and Tom Poston (far right).

Also attending this important Universal International import opening is Jessica Tandy and her daughter (*left*) and Lee Remick (*right*).

FAMOUS BIRTHS

ANTONIO BANDERAS

KENNETH BRANAGH

HUGH GRANT

DARYL HANNAH

TIMOTHY HUTTON

CATHY MORIARTY

SEAN PENN

JAMES SPADER

KRISTIN SCOTT THOMAS

MEG TILLY

STANLEY TUCCI

JEAN-CLAUDE VAN DAMME

STARS
OF TOMORROW

Warren Beatty
Stephen Boyd
Horst Buchholz
James Darren
Angie Dickinson
Troy Donohue
Fabian
John Gavin
George Hamilton
Dolores Hart
Susan Kohner
Nancy Kwan
Juliet Prowse
Tuesday Weld

Hey Let's Get Drunk At Sardi's

Known for his rather boisterous behavior Brendan Behan, whose play *The Hostage* is opening on Broadway, is the first person ever barred in advance from Sherman Billingsley's posh Stork Club.

*In The Meantime…*The Stork Stalks

Celebrities responding to an Actors Equity Association telegram in regard to a labor dispute between Billingsley and his employees boycott the famous Stork resulting in a $5 million lawsuit against Actors Equity.

Juliet Prowse, on loan from 20th Century Fox, is signed by Hal Wallis to play opposite Elvis Presley in "G.I. Blues."

TEENAGERS PICK THEIR FAVORITE MOVIE STARS

Cary Grant

Debbie Reynolds

THE BOX OFFICE STARS

Tony Curtis
Doris Day
Sandra Dee
Cary Grant
Rock Hudson
Jack Lemmon
Debbie Reynolds
Frank Sinatra
ElizabethTaylor
John Wayne

WHAT A YEAR IT WAS!

1960

**1960**

A study reveals that 86 out of 100 leading stars come from broken homes.

Who Am I

"My head knocks against the stars. My feet are on the hilltops..."

Poet **Carl Sandburg** arrives in Hollywood to collaborate with director **George Stevens** on "The Greatest Story Ever Told."

Hauled into court by his fourth wife, **Elaine Davis**, **Mickey Rooney** testifies that he is $175,000 in debt.

WHEN MOSES SPEAKS, THE STUDIO LISTENS

Screen Writers Guild goes on a 3-day strike along with Screen Actors Guild over sharing in studio profits from sale of post 1948 films, with an agreement negotiated between studio executives and **Ronald Reagan** and **Charlton Heston** representing SAG.

PASSINGS

The most beloved movie star of his generation, **CLARK GABLE** is dead at 59 from a heart attack only weeks after finishing his last picture, "The Misfits." The king of cinema and former oil field worker won an Academy Award for "It Happened One Night" and uttered the most immortal line in movie history, "Frankly my dear, I don't give a damn." Gable leaves behind wife Kay Spreckels, pregnant with his first child.

Member of the famed theatrical Barrymore family, **DIANA BARRYMORE** dies at 38 from a barbiturate overdose.

Filmmaker **MACK SENNETT**, who originated slapstick and the Keystone Cops, made 1,000 movies and turned Charlie Chaplin, Buster Keaton and Gloria Swanson into stars, dies at age 80.

I'M MOST EXPENSIVE, NO I'M MOST EXPENSIVE, NO, I'M MOST EXPENSIVE

The biggest and one of the most expensive films in motion picture history, *Spartacus* is shot using the newest process of filming – Super Technirama-70, developed by Technicolor.

BARGING DOWN THE RIVER TO THE TUNE OF ABOUT $2,800,000

Lloyd's of London is faced with the largest claim ever made against the insurers of a film when "Cleopatra" star Elizabeth Taylor is laid up for four weeks after developing Malta fever which she contracted through goat's milk while taking a holiday in the Greek Islands.

1960 POPULAR SONGS

A Thousand Stars...................... *Kathy Young with*
The Innocents
Alley-Oop.................................. *Hollywood Argyles*
Are You Lonesome Tonight?.... *Elvis Presley*
Artificial Flowers .... *Bobby Darin*
Baby (You Got What It Takes) *Dinah Washington*
& Brook Benton
Baby It's Cold Outside .... *Ray Charles &*
Betty Carter
Bill Bailey................................. *Bobby Darin*
Bye Bye Baby .... *Mary Wells*
(1st Motown single to hit the U.S. Hot 100)
Cathy's Clown .... *Everly Brothers*
Chain Gang............................... *Sam Cooke*
Clementine................................ *Bobby Darin*
Corinna, Corinna...................... *Ray Peterson*
Devil Or Angel.......................... *Bobby Vee*
Finger Poppin' Time................ *Hank Ballard &*
The Midnighters
Footsteps .... *Steve Lawrence*
Georgia On My Mind.............. *Ray Charles*
Greenfields................................ *Brothers Four*
Handy Man................................ *Jimmy Jones*
Harbor Lights............................ *The Platters*
He'll Have To Stay .... *Jeanne Black*
The Hucklebuck........................ *Chubby Checker*
I Want To Be Wanted .... *Brenda Lee*
I'm Sorry .... *Brenda Lee*
It's Now Or Never..................... *Elvis Presley*
Itsy Bitsy Teenie Weenie Yellow Polka-Dot Bikini
.... *Brian Hyland*
Last Date.................................. *Floyd Cramer*
Lonely Teenager .... *Dion*
Mama .... *Connie Francis*
Mr. Custer................................. *Larry Verne*
Mule Skinner Blues .... *The Fendermen*
My Girl Josephine .... *Fats Domino*

My Heart Has A Mind Of Its Own. *Connie Francis*
My Home Town .... *Paul Anka*
Ol' MacDonald .... *Frank Sinatra*
Only The Lonely .... *Roy Orbison*
Perfidia..................................... *The Ventures*
Peter Gunn .... *Duane Eddy*
Pineapple Princess .... *Annette with*
The Afterbeats
Poetry In Motion...................... *Johnny Tillotson*
Puppy Love................................ *Paul Anka*
Running Bear .... *Johnny Preston*
Save The Last Dance For Me .. *The Drifters*
Sixteen Reasons........................ *Connie Stevens*
So Sad (To Watch Good Love Go Bad) .. *Everly Brothers*
Stairway To Heaven................... *Neil Sedaka*
Stay.. *Maurice Williams*
& The Zodiacs
Stuck On You............................ *Elvis Presley*
Sway .... *Bobby Rydell*
Swingin' School .... *Bobby Rydell*
Teen Angel .... *Mark Dinning*
That's All You Gotta Do .... *Brenda Lee*
Theme From A Summer Place. *Percy Faith*
Three Nights A Week................ *Fats Domino*
The Twist .... *Chubby Checker*
Walk-Don't Run....................... *The Ventures*
When Will I Be Loved?........... *Everly Brothers*
White Christmas .... *Bing Crosby*
White Silver Sands................... *Bill Black's Combo*
Wild One................................... *Bobby Rydell*
Will You Love Me Tomorrow .. *The Shirelles*
Wonderful World .... *Sam Cooke*
Wonderland By Night............... *Burt Kaempfert*
You Talk Too Much.................. *Joe Jones*
You Were Made For All My Love. *Jackie Wilson*
Young Emotions .... *Ricky Nelson*
You're Sixteen .... *Johnny Burnette*

Shop here for "The Gift That Keeps On Giving"!

THE STARFLAIR table radio

THE SPORTFLAIR table radio

THE GALAHAD AM-FM table radio

THE CONSUL FM table radio

THE FORMFLAIR clock-radio

THE DREAMFLAIR clock-radio

THE TRIMFLAIR clock-radio

THE TRIBUNE cordless clock-radio

THE ENSIGN transistor portable

TRAVEL TWINS radio plus alarm clock

GLOBE TROTTER transistor portable

"POCKETTE" PERSONAL Gift Pack

RCA Victor radios are priced as low as $19.95

Give the most <u>beautiful</u> radios you've ever heard! RCA VICTOR radios!

Flairline-styled table and clock radios—many *almost 4 inches thin!* Brilliantly designed AM-FM and FM radios, some models with AFC (Automatic Frequency Control)! AFC locks FM stations in tune, gives you static-free reception! Radios with "Filteramic" Antenna screen man-made static! *All* with exclusive RCA Victor "Golden Throat" tone! See your RCA Victor dealer!

Nationally advertised list price shown, optional with dealer. Slightly higher West, South. Price, specifications subject to change.   Tmk(s)®

RCA The Most Trusted Name in Radio

RADIO CORPORATION OF AMERICA

THE CHARMFLAIR. Flairline-styled new table radio—almost 4 inches thin! Exclusive "Filteramic" Antenna screens household static. Shell white and three lovely two-tone color combinations.

 # IT'S COUNTRY

Carmel By The Sea	*Kitty Wells*
Crying My Heart Out Over You	*Flatt & Scruggs*
Drifting Texas Sand	*Webb Pierce*
Ev'rybody's Somebody's Fool	*Ernest Tubb*
He'll Have To Go	*Jim Reeves*
Here I Am Drunk Again	*Clyde Beavers*
I'm A Honky Tonk Girl	*Loretta Lynn*
I've Got A Right To Know	*Buck Owens*
Mean Eyed Cat	*Johnny Cash*
Out Of Control	*George Jones*
Polka On A Banjo	*Flatt & Scruggs*
Seasons Of My Heart	*Johnny Cash*
Straight A's In Love	*Johnny Cash*

HE'S ON THE ROAD AGAIN

Country Music Poet **WILLIE NELSON** moves to Nashville and hangs out at Tootsie's Orchid Lounge with other songwriters including **HANK COCHRAN, MEL TILLIS, ROGER MILLER** and **KRIS KRISTOFFERSON**.

EL PASO *is the first Country & Western song to win a Grammy.*

THE STATLER BROTHERS, *neither Statlers nor brothers, reorganize when Don Reid joins his brother Harold.*

FOLK MUSIC'S POPULAR or UP-AND-COMING Names

Odetta
Theodore Bikel
Pete Seeger
The Weavers
Joan Baez

FINGER-PICKIN' GOOD

Banjo Bars *proliferate in San Francisco.*

THIS LAND IS YOUR LAND

Banjoist/balladeer **Pete Seeger** *performs a 2-hour program of international folk music at Hollywood High School benefit for the Youth Guidance League.*

LET'S CUT THE TWIST AND JUST SHOUT

The Newport Folk Festival which includes **Lester Flatt** *and* **Earl Scruggs, Joan Baez** *and* **Pete Seeger** *ends with a Hootenanny inviting audience members to get on stage and hoot and holler.*

 WHAT A YEAR IT WAS!

GRAMMY awards

song of the year
Theme from "Exodus" Ernest Gold, songwriter

record of the year
Theme from "A Summer Place" Percy Faith

album of the year
The Button Down Mind Of Bob Newhart

new artist
Bob Newhart

male vocal performance
Georgia On My Mind (single) Ray Charles

female vocal performance
Mack The Knife (single) Ella Fitzgerald

vocal group
We Got Us Steve Lawrence, Edyie Gorme

rhythm & blues
Let The Good Times Roll Ray Charles

jazz composition
Sketches Of Spain Miles Davis and Gil Evans

country & western
El Paso Marty Robbins

new to the recording scene

Joan Baez   **Gary "U.S." Bonds**
Jerry Butler   **Dion**
Ferrante & Teicher

SLOW CRAWL INTO FAME

The Beatles tour Scotland with British Rock star Johnny Gentle after failing an audition to become Billy Fury's back-up band.

The Beatles give first performance in Hamburg, West Germany in a striptease bar.

hit albums

The Sound Of Music

Inside Shelley Berman

Heavenly Johnny Mathis

Elvis Is Back

Nice 'n' Easy Frank Sinatra

The Wonderful World Of Jonathan Winters

The Ebullient Mr. Gillespie Dizzy Gillespie

Mort Sahl At The Hungry i

TWIST AND SHOUT

Chubby Checker introduces **the Twist** and popularizes it on **Dick Clark's "American Bandstand."** Checker isn't the originator of the song that spawns the great dance craze. That honor belongs to **Hank Ballard** who wrote and recorded the tune as the "B" side of his 1958 hit *"Teardrops On My Letter."*

Will You Love Me Tomorrow tops the charts making **The Shirelles** the first female group to record a no. 1 single.

Gladys Knight makes her professional recording debut at age 16 with her group, **Gladys Knight & The Pips**.

Sam Cooke signs with **RCA**.

18-year old gospel singer **Aretha Franklin** makes her first secular recordings for producer **John Hammond** at **Columbia Records**.

Smokey Robinson & The Miracles put **Motown** on the map with the label's first million seller record— *Shop Around*.

Clockwise, Smokey Robinson, Sam Cooke, Aretha Franklin

WHAT A YEAR IT WAS!

The Fans Are All Washed Up

Los Cerrillos airport in Santiago, Chile sustains $25,000 in damages as hysterical bobby-soxers are doused with water hoses as they converge to greet Canadian Rock 'n' Roll singer **Paul Anka**.

At age 18, **Paul Anka** is the youngest performer to play the famous Copacabana nightclub in New York.

Despite his **Not Guilty** plea, DJ **Alan Freed** is indicted for receiving **$30,650** in **Payola**. **Dick Clark** admits to having a financial interest in 27% of records played on **American Bandstand**.

Victim of the payola scandal **Alan Freed** is replaced by DJ **Clay Cole** at the annual **Christmas Rock & Roll Show** at Brooklyn's Paramount Theatre featuring *Johnny Burnette, Chubby Checker, Bo Diddley, Dion, The Drifters, Bobby Rydell* and *Neil Sedaka*.

Elvis Presley receives his first Gold Album for *Elvis* which includes *Rip It Up, Old Shep* and *Ready Teddy*.

1960

Marlene Dietrich is one of the excited fans who shows up for **Nat "King" Cole's** concert in Paris' Palais de Chaillot where the "King" brings in a staggering $10,000 gross in one night.

Ending On A Discordant Note

The Newport City Council votes to revoke the Newport Jazz Festival's entertainment license after police, National Guard and the U.S. Marines are called in to control 12,000 drunken rioting college students.

GERRY MULLIGAN SAN

A Japanese version of *Down Beat* hits the Tokyo newsstands as coffee houses blast the sounds of **Gerry Mulligan**, **Dizzy Gillespie** and **Thelonious Monk**.

New Man On The Jazz Block

Alto saxophonist **Ornette Coleman**, touted as the only one doing something new in jazz since the mid '40's, is packing them in at Greenwich Village's Five Spot Café.

THE "REAL" KING OF JAZZ

Jazz musician **King Bhumibol** of Thailand sits in on a jam session with **Benny Goodman** during his visit to the U.S.

Summer Jazz In The City

New York's Museum of Modern Art kicks off its Patio Jazz Series with blues singer **Jimmy Rushing** and the **Joe Newman** Sextet.

BAREFOOT & PREGNANT MOST OF THE TIME

Jose Ferrer's wife **Rosemary Clooney**, pregnant five times in her seven year marriage, performs at the Empire Room at New York's Waldorf Astoria, the first time she's sung on a New York stage in nine years.

GRAMMY'S ON HIS MIND

Ray Charles has four standards in the Hot 100 — *Come Rain Or Come Shine, Ruby, Hard Hearted Hannah* and the Grammy-winning *Georgia On My Mind*.

A ROYAL VISIT

American's leading composer-bandleader, **Duke Ellington**, performs at the Santa Monica Civic Auditorium.

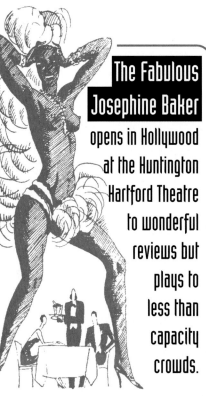

The Fabulous Josephine Baker opens in Hollywood at the Huntington Hartford Theatre to wonderful reviews but plays to less than capacity crowds.

MAHALIA STORMS WASHINGTON, D.C.

World's greatest gospel singer, **Mahalia Jackson**, tapes a program for the Voice of America, gives a hand-clapping concert in the Daughters of the American Revolution concert hall and is honored at a reception at the Georgetown home of Representative Chester Bowles.

THE HIGH PRICE OF BORSCHT

Singer **Billy Eckstein** flies in from Casablanca to perform for one night only in the Catskill Mountains at the Concord Hotel's Imperial Room, one of the world's largest nightclubs, for a four figure salary.

WHAT A YEAR IT WAS!

HEY, LET'S CUT THE CLOWNING

"Cathy's Clown," the **Everly Brothers'** first release on Warner Brothers label, is an international hit.

The **Everly Brothers** kick off their first British tour performing in London.

TEENS REIGN SUPREME

Teenagers hitting the top of the charts include **Brenda Lee**, 15, **Chubby Checker**, 19, **Bryan Hyland**, 16 and **Paul Anka**, 18.

Billboard reports that the average teenage girl spends 4 1/2 hours every day listening to pop music.

The PRESIDENT Meets The CHAIRMAN And His CABINET

With presidential hopeful **John F. Kennedy** ringside, **Frank Sinatra, Dean Martin, Sammy Davis, Jr., Peter Lawford** and **Joey Bishop** put on a spectacular show at the Sands Hotel in Las Vegas.

THE TACKLE TACKLES TONSORIAL TONES

Rosey Grier, New York Giants' defensive 6'5" 285-pound tackle, sings at New York's Town Hall.

THEY'VE GOT HIM UNDER THEIR SKIN

THE METROPOLITAN OPERA HOUSE holds a salute to COLE PORTER, one of America's most distinguished geniuses of the musical theatre, celebrating his 50th anniversary as a songwriter.

HIS TIME IS YOUR TIME

Rudy Vallee, sans a megaphone, performs at New York's Roundtable supper club announcing that he is "...the Pat Boone of the Stone Age..."

A celebrity-filled audience shouts accolades as 27-year old Xosa African tribeswoman **Miriam Makeba** makes a riveting debut at New York's Blue Angel supper club.

PASSINGS

Chairman of Steinway & Sons, **WILLIAM R. STEINWAY** dies at age 78.

Rock 'n' roll singer **EDDIE COCHRAN** dies in a London auto accident, while country singer **JOHNNY HORTON** dies in a Texas car crash.

A.P. CARTER, patriarch of the legendary first family of country music, The Carter Family, dies at age 69.

FAMOUS BIRTHS

Bono

Sarah Brightman

Branford Marsalis

Michael Stipe

AT LAST, IT'S EASY TO TAKE GREAT MOVIES INDOORS

NEW SYLVANIA **SUN GUN MOVIE LIGHT**

Only $**24**^95 *

DOES AWAY WITH BULKY BAR LIGHTS FOREVER! Now all you need to take great movies indoors is your camera and a compact new SUN GUN movie light.

Though only a handful, this powerful new light brightens the scene like the sun. No double shadows. No overexposed "hot spots." And actors can look close to the camera without squinting. Colors come out more lifelike, too.

Your house is full of wonderful movies . . . waiting to be taken. See the new SUN GUN at your camera counter now. The sun never sets on the man who owns a SUN GUN. Sylvania Lighting Products, 1740 Broadway, New York 19, N. Y.

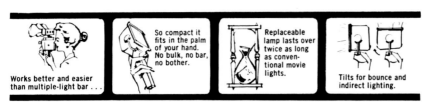

Works better and easier than multiple-light bar . . .

So compact it fits in the palm of your hand. No bulk, no bar, no bother.

Replaceable lamp lasts over twice as long as conventional movie lights.

Tilts for bounce and indirect lighting.

SYLVANIA

Subsidiary of **GENERAL TELEPHONE & ELECTRONICS**

*Manufacturer's suggested list

TELEVISION — 1960

In direct response to the quiz show scandal, the U.S. House of Representatives passes a bill designed to tighten regulations against deceptive broadcasting practices.

PAAR
GOES OFF HIS COURSE

Furious over NBC's censoring of a water closet joke, in a tearful farewell to a stunned audience, **Jack Paar** walks off "The Tonight Show."

BLUE SUEDE SHOES
ARE DANCIN' AGAIN

Fresh out of the service, Elvis makes his first post-Army TV appearance on Frank Sinatra's May ABC-TV special.

WHAT A YEAR IT WAS!

SHOWS

DRAMA
Playhouse 90

HUMOR
VIP–Art Carney Special

VARIETY
The Fabulous Fifties

PERFORMERS

SERIES
Jane Wyatt
"Father Knows Best"
Robert Stack
"The Untouchables"

SINGLE PERFORMANCE
Laurence Olivier
"The Moon And Sixpence"
Ingrid Bergman
"The Turn Of The Screw"
Harry Belafonte
"Tonight With Belafonte"
(1st Negro to win)

1960 EMMY AWARDS

Harry Belafonte

HE DOESN'T LOVE LUCY ANYMORE

Bringing to an end the marriage shared by millions of television viewers since 1951, Lucille Ball and Desi Arnaz file for divorce.

SOMETHING TO WRITE ABOUT

After a five-month strike of the Writers Guild of America which impacted on thousands of actors, crewmen and technicians, a settlement is reached with the Alliance of TV Film Producers and the 775 active writers go back to their typewriters.

1960

NEW SHOWS ON THE TV BLOCK

The Andy Griffith Show

The Bugs Bunny Show

The Flintstones

Matty's Funday Funnies

My Three Sons

Route 66

Surfside Six

The Tall Man

Fred and Wilma Flintstone and their neighbors Barney and Betty Rubble become stars of prime-time television's first animated sitcom – THE FLINTSTONES.

the doctor says no!

MGM-TV has a few restrictions in its search for sponsors for its *Dr. Kildare* series starring Lew Ayres as the "chief of staff" refuses to allow any beer or cigarette advertising on the show.

There's Big Money In Them There Murders

MGM-TV buys the television rights to 60 novels and 200 short stories written by *Agatha Christie* for $1 million plus royalties and residuals.

TOP RATED
TELEVISION PROGRAMS
(AVERAGE FOR 1960)

Gunsmoke

Wagon Train

Have Gun, Will Travel

77 Sunset Strip

Checkmate (Series Premiere)

The Ed Sullivan Show

Perry Mason

The Red Skelton Show

The Price Is Right

I've Got A Secret

The Danny Thomas Show

OLD WOODEN HEAD BITES THE SAWDUST

The Howdy Doody Show which began broadcasting in 1947 goes off the air after 13 seasons and more than 2,500 programs.

WHAT'S UP DOC?

Bugs Bunny, **Daffy Duck**, **Tweet Sylvester** and **Porky Pig** are among the cartoon stars featured on a new prime-time television series.

WHAT A YEAR IT WAS!

116

What's Playing On TV This Week (A SAMPLING)

The Adventures Of Ellery Queen

The Adventures
   Of Ozzie & Harriet

Alcoa Presents

Alfred Hitchcock Presents

The Andy Williams Show

The Ann Sothern Show

Armstrong Circle Theatre

Arthur Murray Party

Bachelor Father

The Barbara Stanwyck Show

Bat Masterson

The Betty Hutton Show

Blondie

Bonanza

Broken Arrow

Candid Camera

The Charlie Farrell Show

Cheyenne

Colt .45

Concentration

December Bride

Dennis The Menace

The Detectives

Dick Powell's Zane Grey Theatre

The Dinah Shore Chevy Show

The Donna Reed Show

Dragnet

Father Knows Best

Fireside Theatre

Frontier Justice

The Gale Storm Show

The George Gobel Show

Hawaiian Eye

The Honeymooners

The Invisible Man

The Jack Benny Show

Jackpot Bowling Starring Milton Berle

Johnny Ringo

Johnny Staccato

The Kate Smith Show

Laramie

Lassie

The Lawless Years

The Lawrence Welk Show

Leave It To Beaver

The Liberace Show

The Life And Legend Of Wyatt Earp

The Loretta Young Show

Lucy In Connecticut

Man From Interpol

The Many Loves Of Dobie Gillis

Maverick

The Millionaire

Mr. Lucky

My Sister Eileen

Naked City

National Velvet

The Outlaws

Ozark Jubilee

The Pat Boone-Chevy Showroom

The Perry Como Show

Person To Person

Peter Gunn

Peter Loves Mary

Playhouse 90

The Porter Wagoner Show

Rawhide

The Real McCoys

Richard Diamond, Private Detective

The Rifleman

Ripley's Believe It Or Not

Sea Hunt

The Shari Lewis Show

Shirley Temple's Storybook

Somerset Maugham Hour

The Spike Jones Show

Steve Canyon

The Tab Hunter Show

Tales Of Wells Fargo

The Texan

This Is Your Life

Thriller

The Tom Ewell Show

The Walter Winchell Show

The Westerner

Winston Churchill: The Valiant Years

The Witness

Jack Benny

Lassie

Betty Hutton

WHAT A YEAR IT WAS!

1960

FACES SEEN ON THE BOOB TUBE

Clint Eastwood
James Garner
Jackie Gleason
Peter Graves
Lorne Greene
Merv Griffin
Buddy Hackett
Florence
   Henderson
Ronny Howard
Tab Hunter
David Janssen

Edie Adams
Desi Arnaz
Fred Astaire
Lucille Ball
Warren Beatty
Polly Bergen
Walter Brennan
Lloyd Bridges
Charles Bronson
Raymond Burr
Chuck Connors
Richard Crenna
Troy Donahue

Boris Karloff
Brian Keith

Gene Kelly
Don Knotts
Ernie Kovacs
Michael Landon
Jerry Lewis
Fred MacMurray
Groucho Marx
Darren McGavin
Steve McQueen
Ray Milland
Martin Milner
Roger Moore
Edward R. Murrow
Vincent Price
Burt Reynolds
Wayne Rogers
Mort Sahl
Robert Stack
Tuesday Weld
Betty White
Efrem Zimbalist, Jr.

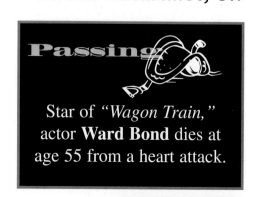

Passing

Star of *"Wagon Train,"* actor **Ward Bond** dies at age 55 from a heart attack.

WHAT A YEAR IT WAS!

siontelevision

1960

ALAN WATTS, the most visible exponent of Eastern religions, and Zen Buddhism in particular, hosts a National Education Television series entitled *Eastern Wisdom And Modern Life*.

famous births

valerie BERTINELLI

RuPAUL

david DUCHOVNY

damon WAYANS

Let Me Say This About That – As To Which Is More Telegenic, My Left Side Is Definitely Better Than My Right Side

New ground in presidential campaigning is broken as candidates John F. Kennedy and Richard Nixon engage in four nationally televised "great debates."

THE GROWING OF THE VAST WASTELAND

As of May, there are an estimated 52,500,000 million television sets in American homes.

EUGENE O'NEILL's play ***The Iceman Cometh*** starring Jason Robards and Robert Redford premieres on television.

RADIO DAYS

THE DEATH OF THE SOAPS

Helen Trent is romanced for the last time, *Ma Perkins* bids her audience a fond adieu after 27 years, *Young Dr. Malone* has to find another hospital and *The Second Mrs. Burton* can tell no more tales as CBS ends its broadcast of daytime soaps becoming the last network to end this long-running, popular programming format.

One of radio's first all-night disk jockey shows, MILKMAN'S MATINEE, *celebrates its 25th anniversary.*

THE LAST STRAW

Louisiana Hayride
goes off the air.

WHAT A YEAR IT WAS!

▲ The gift nobody could give before

First big-screen all-transistor portable you don't have to plug in

This is the new Motorola portable—forerunner of all TV to come and gift idea of a lifetime.

It plays anywhere there's a signal: indoors on ordinary house current; outdoors on its amazing *rechargeable* energy cell. Its face is practically all picture—thanks to the new 19-inch Picture Frame Screen (over-all diag. meas.; 172 sq. in. viewing area).

The result of five years' research and development, it has no tubes. Instead it uses transistors (the miracle of the missile age) that last indefinitely to establish new standards in TV performance and reliability.

Choose (or hint for) the first Portable TV truly designed to be a portable. It will be liked as long as it's looked at—for years to come! Available exclusively at your Motorola dealer's.

Compact and trim, new portable looks like finest luggage, has removable screen cover. In Tahiti Tan or Black Onyx, trimmed in polished chrome. Available with UHF tuning.

 MOTOROLA

SPECIFICATIONS SUBJECT TO CHANGE WITHOUT NOTICE.

ON BROADWAY

THE SHOW DOESN'T GO ON

ACTORS EQUITY CALLS A STRIKE AGAINST THE
LEAGUE OF NEW YORK THEATRES AND BROADWAY
IS DARK FOR TEN DAYS~
THE FIRST TIME SINCE
THE 1919
GREAT FLU
EPIDEMIC.

Chita
Rivera and
Dick
Van Dyke
in
*Bye
Bye
Birdie*

ANOTHER OPENING, ANOTHER NIGHT

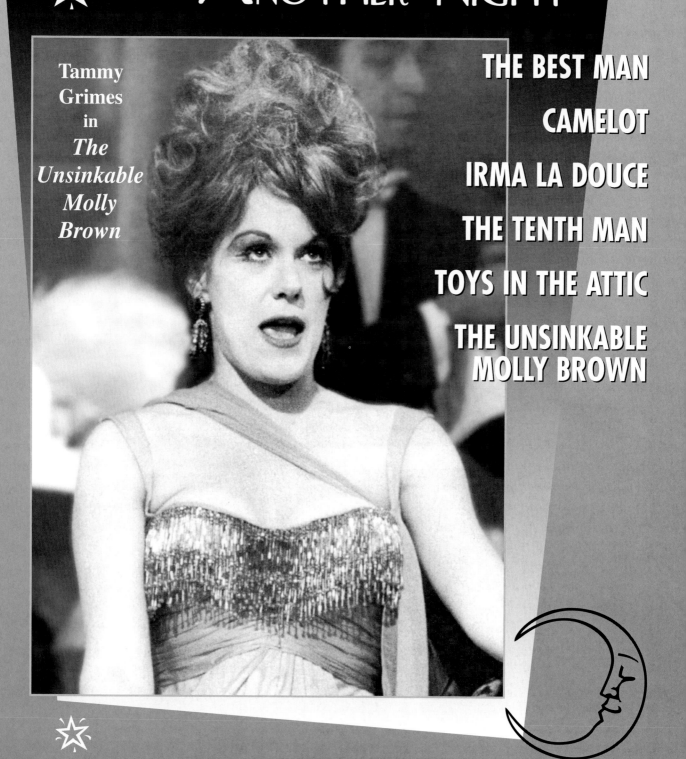

Tammy Grimes in *The Unsinkable Molly Brown*

THE BEST MAN

CAMELOT

IRMA LA DOUCE

THE TENTH MAN

TOYS IN THE ATTIC

THE UNSINKABLE MOLLY BROWN

WHAT ELSE IS PLAYING:

A Taste Of Honey

✿

A Thurber Carnival

✿

Advise And Consent

✿

All The Way Home

✿

An Evening With Mike Nichols And Elaine May

✿

The Balcony

✿

Becket

✿

Caligula

✿

Critic's Choice

✿

The Deadly Game

✿

Dear Liar

✿

Five Finger Exercise

OFF BROADWAY OPENINGS:

1960

The Fantasticks	**(Tom Jones & Harvey Schmidt)**
Time Of Vengeance	**(Ugo Betti)**
The Killer	**(Eugene Ionesco)**
Krapp's Last Tape	**(Samuel Beckett)**

The American Shakespeare Festival kicks off its season in Stratford, Connecticut with **Katharine Hepburn** starring in *Twelfth Night*.

FAMOUS BIRTH
Lee Michael Cohn

Never Give Up Your Dream

Fulfilling a life-long dream to be on stage, 65-year old **James Thurber** joins Actors Equity as a junior member and appears on Broadway in his own hit revue *A Thurber Carnival*.

No Need To Invent A Better Mousetrap

Agatha Christie's *The Mousetrap* becomes the longest running play in the history of British theatre.

Eugene Ionesco's play rhinoceros premieres in Paris.

Tony Awards
1960

OUTSTANDING PLAY
"The Miracle Worker"
William Gibson (playwright)

OUTSTANDING MUSICAL
"Fiorello!"
"The Sound Of Music"

OUTSTANDING DRAMATIC ACTOR
Melvyn Douglas
"The Best Man"

OUTSTANDING DRAMATIC ACTRESS
Anne Bancroft
"The Miracle Worker"

OUTSTANDING DIRECTOR
Arthur Penn
"The Miracle Worker"

OUTSTANDING MUSICAL ACTOR
Jackie Gleason
"Take Me Along"

OUTSTANDING MUSICAL ACTRESS
Mary Martin
"The Sound Of Music"

OUTSTANDING DIRECTOR - MUSICAL
George Abbott
"Fiorello!"

OUTSTANDING CHOREOGRAPHER
Michael Kidd
"Destry Rides Again"

SPECIAL AWARDS
John D. Rockefeller III for vision and leadership in creating Lincoln Center, a landmark of theatre encompassing the performing arts.

James Thurber and **Burgess Meredith** for "A Thurber Carnival."

Tom Thatcher, Patty Duke and Patricia Neal in *The Miracle Worker*

OBIE SPEAKS
Jack Gelber's **The Connection** wins an Obie prize as best new play while Jack Richardson's **The Prodigal** and newcomer Edward Albee's **The Zoo Story** are cited as "distinguished plays" — the first produced works for Richardson and Albee.

THE PRETTY REDHEAD IS LEFT HOLDING THE BATON

Liza Redfield successfully conducts *The Music Man* becoming Broadway's first full-time female conductor.

Actors Equity fines 28-year old **John Barrymore, Jr.** $5,000 and a year's suspension from the American stage for walking out on a road company production of *Look Homeward Angel*.

WHAT A YEAR IT WAS!

WHAT ELSE IS PLAYING:

Henry IV, Part I

☆

Henry IV, Part II

☆

The Hostage

☆

Invitation To A March

☆

Little Mary Sunshine

☆

Little Moon Of Alban

☆

Once Upon A Mattress

☆

Period Of Adjustment

☆

The Prodigal

☆

Silent Night, Lonely Night

☆

The Sound Of Music

☆

Under The Yum-Yum Tree

flops galore

The Tumbler, directed by **Laurence Olivier** and starring **Charlton Heston, Rosemary Harris** and **Martha Scott**, becomes the sixth Broadway production to open and close within a week during the month of February.

they could have clapped all night

American performance of **My Fair Lady** in Moscow receives standing ovation from sell-out crowd.

the comrades keep the cash

American playwright **Arthur Miller** is less than excited on learning that a Moscow publisher is printing a book of his plays including **Death Of A Salesman** and **View From The Bridge** as Russia thinks it's unfashionable to pay royalties to foreigners.

hark, is that a stage i see in yon distance?

Joseph Papp brings free Shakespeare performances to New York City's Central Park.

PASSINGS

Lyricist **Oscar Hammerstein II**, who along with partner Richard Rodgers, forever changed musical comedy, dies at age 65. *Oklahoma!, South Pacific, The King and I, Carousel, The Sound of Music* and *Show Boat* all bear Hammerstein's talented touch. During his long and illustrious career, he won an Academy Award, Pulitzer Prize and New York Drama Critics' Circle Award.

Barbiturates take the life of 48-year old Broadway star **Margaret Sullavan**, who was starring in the play *Sweet Love Remember'd* at the time of her death.

The real inspiration for Peter Pan, **Peter L. Davies** dies at age 68 after being hit by a London subway train.

Dance

Lady From The Sea, a new ballet choreographed by **Birgit Cullberg,** premieres at the Metropolitan Opera House to critical acclaim.

Dancers *from the Ballet Russe de Monte Carlo,* which include over a dozen Americans, perform in Santa Monica, California for the first time.

Choreographer **Frederick Ashton** presents the U.S. premiere of *Ondine,* thought to be his most ambitious work to date.

Modern *dancer* **Jose Limon** tours South America under the auspices of the U.S. State Department.

Former *Sadler's Wells ballerina* and star of *The Red Shoes,* **Moira Shearer** comes out of retirement at 34 and dances Roxanne with elegance and grace in a movie version of **Roland Petit's** *Cyrano de Bergerac* being shot in Paris.

Former *Martha Graham dancer-choreographer* **Merce Cunningham** premieres two pieces, *Summerspace* and *Antic Meet,* with music by **Morton Feldman** and **John Cage,** respectively.

Critics *laud Preludios Para Percusion,* music composed by **Luis Escobar** of Colombia and *Variaciones Concertantes,* music composed by **Alberto Ginastera** of Argentina — two of eight new works presented under New York City Ballet's *Panamerica* project dedicated to New York Governor **Nelson A. Rockefeller.**

WHAT IS THIS MADNESS?

Set to the music of **Duke Ellington,** choreographer **Maurice Bejart's "Such Sweet Thunder,"** performed at Brussels' Royal Opera House, is critically panned as one of the most deranged ballets ever staged.

THE KANGAROO BOUNCE

CBS television commissions composer **Igor Stravinsky** and choreographer **George Balanchine** to create a ballet based on the biblical story of Noah.

He's Dancing And Singing In The Rain In Paris

Choreographing to the music of **George Gershwin, Gene Kelly** stages "Pas des Dieux," the first jazz ballet ever staged at the Paris Opera making him the first American allowed this privilege.

Great Britain-originated Ballroom Dancing becomes more popular in the U.S.

THE RUSSIANS SAY *"DA"*

American Ballet Theatre featuring internationally known prima ballerina **Maria Tallchief** becomes first U.S. dance company to tour the Soviet Union.

HEY, IS SHE MAKING FUN OF CLASSICAL BALLET?

Martha Graham's tongue-in-cheek *Acrobats of God,* first ballet of her new dance season, meets with critical confusion as to her intention.

NO STANDING ROOM ONLY

All performances by Britain's Royal Ballet at the Metropolitan Opera House are virtually sold out before the box-office even opens thanks to promoter **Sol Hurok's** announcement that tickets could be ordered by mail.

A MAGIC CARPET RIDE

New York City Ballet's **George Balanchine** premieres *The Figure In The Carpet,* critics calling it his most ambitious work since *Nutcracker.*

126

WHAT A YEAR IT WAS!

1960

Classical Music

Benjamin Britten

conducts the first performance of his operatic version of *A Midsummer Night's Dream* in Aldeburgh, England.

Dmitri Shostakovich

receives standing ovation after conducting his new compositon *Concerto for Cello* at London's Royal Festival Hall.

A Story of a Real Man a new opera by **Sergei Prokofiev** gets a world premiere at the Bolshoi Theatre in Moscow.

▶

Igor Stravinsky

conducts the first performance of his *Monumentum pro Gesualdo di Venosa ad CD Annum* at the 23rd Festival Of Contemporary Music in Venice.

The Imperial Classic Stereophonic High Fidelity with FM/AM radio. Choice of fine woods ... $650.00

THRILL TO THE WORLD'S FINEST STEREOPHONIC HIGH FIDELITY— for music becomes magic when Magnavox sets it free. New Magnavox developments enable you to enjoy incredible fidelity and sound "separation." Each instrument stands out with brilliant clarity—you can "see" its location in the orchestra, you can feel the full depth and sweep of sound. You are literally surrounded by the breathtaking realism of a live performance. Here is music recreated as the artist or conductor himself would wish it—one reason so many of them own a Magnavox. Let your Magnavox Dealer, listed in the Yellow Pages, show you why Magnavox is the finest ... and your best buy on *any* basis of comparison. Other consoles from $139.50. the magnificent **Magnavox**

WORLD LEADER IN STEREOPHONIC HIGH FIDELITY AND QUALITY TELEVISION

New Works

Portrait de Mallarme
Pierre Boulez

Der Prinz von Homburg
An Opera By Hans Werner Henze

Rosamunde Floris
An Opera By Boris Blacher

Fourth Symphony
Roger Sessions

Movements for Piano and Orchestra Igor Stravinsky

Spectra Gunther Schuller

Ninth Symphony Milhaud

San Francisco Suite
Ferde Grofe

Missa Pro Defunctis
Virgil Thomson

Cantata Academica
Benjamin Britten

Toccata Festiva Samuel Barber

Seventh Symphony
William Schuman

The Salzburg Music Festival, one of Europe's most important festivals, opens its concert season with a brand new *Festspielhaus*, reputed to be the world's most technically advanced theatre.

American audiences get their first opportunity to hear a Russian symphony as the Moscow State Symphony begins a 20-city tour with a concert in New York City.

Pulitzer Prize 1960
Second String Quartet
Elliott Carter

LEOPOLD STOKOWSKI returns to the podium of the Philadelphia Orchestra after a 19-year exile.

Immediately on returning to New York after a 72-day U.S. and Canadian tour performing 34 concerts, virtuoso violinist ISAAC STERN spearheads a campaign to save New York City's famed Carnegie Hall from the wrecking ball. At the eleventh hour a citizens' committee enables the city to buy the 69-year old music shrine for $5 million.

AARON COPLAND celebrates his 60th birthday by conducting the New York Philharmonic, taping a television program with LEONARD BERNSTEIN and introducing his new book "Copland On Music."

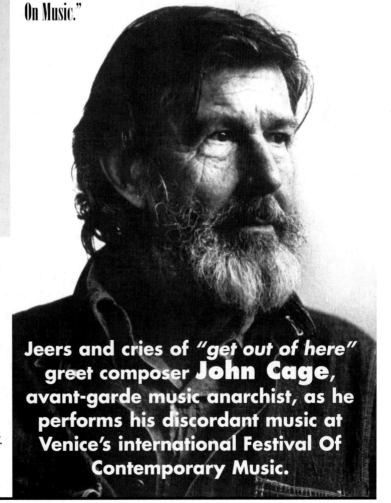

Jeers and cries of *"get out of here"* greet composer **John Cage**, avant-garde music anarchist, as he performs his discordant music at Venice's international Festival Of Contemporary Music.

WHAT A YEAR IT WAS!

1960

Opera News

33-year old American soprano **Leontyne Price** makes her La Scala debut in *Aida*.

Australian soprano **Joan Sutherland** makes her American debut in Handel's *Alcina* at the Dallas Civic Opera.

Opera's bad girl Diva **Maria Callas** is star of La Scala's opening night production of Donizetti's obscure opera *Poliuto*.

• Construction scheduled to begin on the new $32 million Metropolitan Opera House at Lincoln Center with a target completion date of 1963.

• The Met announces that it has optioned an opera based on the 1920's Massachusetts Sacco-Vanzetti sensational murder case.

PASSINGS

The career of one of America's finest opera baritones comes to a tragic end as **Leonard Warren** collapses and dies at age 48 during a performance at the Met of *La Forza del Destino*.

World renowned conductor **Dimitri Mitropoulos** suffers a heart attack and dies during a rehearsal at La Scala. The 64-year old had conducted symphonies and orchestras in Europe and the United States, and at the time of his death was with the Metropolitan Opera in New York.

California-born baritone at the Metropolitan Opera for twenty-five years, **Lawrence Tibbet** dies at age 63.

Tibbet

WHAT A YEAR IT WAS!

At The MUSEUM

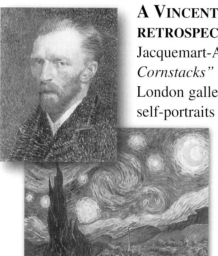

A VINCENT VAN GOGH RETROSPECTIVE at Paris' Musee Jacquemart-Andre includes *"The Cornstacks"* and *"Starry Night."* At a London gallery nearly twenty of his self-portraits are on view, while 160 works tour several Canadian institutions.

The Museum of Modern Art turns 30 and the Los Angeles County Museum turns 50.

IN AN EFFORT TO RAISE MONEY, **THE MUSEUM OF MODERN ART** in New York holds an auction with interested buyers in Los Angeles, Dallas and Chicago participating via closed-circuit television. Celebrated artists such as **Joan Miro, Alberto Giacometti, Jean Dubuffet** and **Henry Moore** donate works. **Cezanne's** *"Apples"* goes for $200,000 and **Braque's** *"The Violin"* brings in $145,000.

CLAUDE MONET'S *"SEASONS AND MOMENTS"* is mounted at New York's Museum of Modern Art and the Los Angeles County Museum.

THE STATE MUSEUM IN STUTTGART, GERMANY acquires over $2 million worth of modern paintings by **Picasso, Modigliani, Bonnard, Matisse, Cezanne** and others.

A MASK EXHIBIT at **Musee Guimet** in Paris includes primitive art from Tibet, Egypt and Greece.

SHOWMAN BILLY ROSE DONATES HIS $1 MILLION SCULPTURE COLLECTION to the National Museum of Israel in Jerusalem. Rose hires **Isamu Noguchi** to create a garden to display the 50+ pieces.

AN ART NOUVEAU SHOW AT THE MUSEUM OF MODERN ART features pieces by **Tiffany** and **Beardsley**.

THE WORCESTER ART MUSEUM presents **Georgia O'Keeffe's** most extensive exhibit ever seen in New England, covering four decades of work.

O'Keeffe

1960

RENOIR'S HOME IN FRANCE is turned into a museum.

GEORGES BRAQUE has a one-man show at the Pasadena Art Museum and is featured at Paris' Bibliotheque Nationale.

> Willem de Kooning, Alexander Calder and Marcel Duchamp are elected to the National Institute of Arts and Letters.

> Marcel Duchamp and Andre Breton coordinate Paris' Eighth International Exhibition of Surrealism. In the U.S., Bennington College in Vermont mounts *"Surrealism: 1913-1946."*

> Marc Chagall and Oskar Kokoschka share the Dutch Erasmus Prize for their contributions to European culture.

> Isamu Noguchi's sculpture *"The Self"* wins 1st Prize at the Art Institute of Chicago's 63rd competition.

> Painter Sir Winston Churchill gives the $20,720 earned at auction for his *"Cork Trees Near Mimizan"* to charity.

PAINTING WITH PABLO

- 268 paintings on view at London's Tate Gallery, some from Picasso's private collection.

- $134,000 paid for his blue period "Femme Accroupie," a record price for a Picasso.

- 29 of his paintings go to auction, earning over $600,000, the most ever spent at one time for a living artist.

- Picasso exhibits are held in Paris and New York.

The International Print Biennial at the Cincinnati Art Museum displays his entire bullfight series (26 aquatints) for the first time.

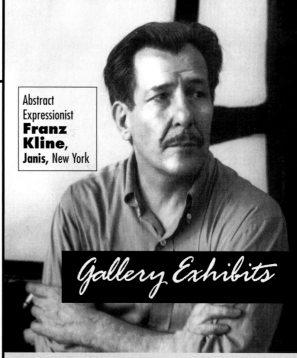

Abstract Expressionist **Franz Kline**, Janis, New York

Gallery Exhibits

Auguste Rodin, Bayer, New York
Cartier-Bresson, IBM, New York
Cecil Beaton, Sagittarius, New York
Edgar Degas, Durand-Ruel, Paris
Elaine de Kooning, Dord Fitz, Amarillo
Fernand Leger, Jeanne Bucher, Paris
Francis Bacon, Marlborough Fine Art, London
Frank Stella, Castelli, New York
Georges Rouault, Perls, New York
Hans Hofmann, Kootz, New York
Henry Moore, Marlborough Fine Art, London
Jacques Lipchitz, Knoedler, New York
James Whistler, Arts Council, London
Jean Arp, Jeanne Bucher, Paris
Jean Dubuffet, Daniel Cordier, Paris
Jim Dine, Reuben, New York
Joan Miro, Beyeler, Basel
Juan Gris, Knoedler, New York
Man Ray, Rive Droit, Paris
Mark Rothko, Neufuille, Paris
Max Ernst, Feigen, Chicago
Paul Gauguin, Charpentier, Paris
Paul Klee, Beveler, Basel
Pierre-Auguste Renoir, Waddington, London
Piet Mondrian, Leicester, London
Richard Diebenkorn, Staempfli, New York
Robert de Niro, Ellison, Fort Worth
Robert Motherwell, Signa, East Hampton
Robert Rauschenberg, Castelli, New York
Wassily Kandinsky, Jeanne Bucher, Paris

WHAT A YEAR IT WAS!

1960 CREATIONS

People In The Sun	**Edward Hopper**	painting
Beer Cans	**Jasper Johns**	sculpture
Ecumenical Council	**Salvador Dali**	painting
Triple Self Portrait	**Norman Rockwell**	painting

A
Jackson Pollock
**painting sells for
over $100,000.**

Happy Birthday, Dear Grandma

Commemorating Grandma Moses' centennial, the Smithsonian sponsors a nationwide tour of her work and Governor Nelson Rockefeller declares her 100th birthday *"Grandma Moses Day"* in New York.

The Philadelphia Museum features a comprehensive **Mary Cassatt** show with some never-before-seen pieces.

The most extensive American showing of Impressionist **Berthe Morisot** is held at Wildenstein's in Manhattan.

Patrons at Jackson Gallery's "New Mediums — New Forms" show can view modern art made from such unusual materials as pillows, trash, newspapers, nails and tacks.

Charges are dropped against the beatnik GAS HOUSE in Venice, California for exhibiting pictures of topless women.

Jasper Johns begins creating lithographs.

In New York art meets theatre as **Claes Oldenburg** performs *"Snapshots From The City"* and **Jim Dine** pours paint on himself in *"The Smiling Workman."*

A famous amateur artists show at Bianchini Gallery includes Henry Fonda, Tallulah Bankhead, Igor Stravinsky, Jerome Robbins, Shirley Booth and Gian-Carlo Menotti.

Auction Highlights

Gainsborough
"Mr. and Mrs. Robert Andrews" $364,000

Rembrandt
"Portrait of a Man" $112,000

Renoir
"Washerwomen" $106,400

Leger
"The Smoker" $ 82,500

PASSING

Creator of the Uncle Sam "I Want You" poster, illustrator **James Montgomery Flagg** dies at age 82.

Dali whips up a new painting in only minutes under the watchful eyes of actress **Joan Crawford** and supreme hostess Perle Mesta.

WHAT A YEAR IT WAS!

1960

Books

A Tourist In Africa
  Evelyn Waugh

A Zoo In My Luggage
  Gerald Durrell

Aimez-vous Brahms
  Francoise Sagan

Baruch: The Public Years
  Bernard M. Baruch

Before You Go
  Jerome Weidman

Between You, Me, and the Gatepost
  Pat Boone

The Big It, And Other Stories
  A.B. Guthrie, Jr.

The Black Book
  Lawrence Durrell

Born Free
  Joy Adamson

Carrington
  Michael Straight

Casanova's Chinese Restaurant
  Anthony Powell

The Chapman Report
  Irving Wallace

The Child Buyer
  John Hersey

Clea
  Lawrence Durrell

Confessions Of An Art Addict
  Peggy Guggenheim

The Constant Image
  Marcia Davenport

Daughter Of The Sky
  Paul L. Briand, Jr.

Daughters And Rebels:
  An Autobiography
  Jessica Mitford

Don't Forget To Write
  Art Buchwald

Dr. Schweitzer of Lambarene
  Norman Cousins

The Edge Of Day
  Laurie Lee

The Four Loves
  C.S. Lewis

Friday's Footprint, And Other Stories
  Nadine Gordimer

Lawrence Durrell

Golk
  Richard G. Stern

Green Eggs And Ham
  Dr. Seuss

Hawaii
  James A. Michener

Homage To Clio
  W.H. Auden

I Kid You Not
  Jack Paar and John Ready

India Today
  F.R. Moraes

In Pursuit Of The English
  Doris Lessing

The Last Of The Just
  Andre Schwarz-Bart

The Last Temptation Of Christ
  Nikos Kazantzakis

The Leopard
  Giuseppe di Lampedusa

The Liberal Hour
  John Kenneth Galbraith

The Light In The Piazza
  Elizabeth Spencer

The Listener
  Taylor Caldwell

Lonesome Traveler
  Jack Kerouac

The Loser
  Peter Ustinov

The Lotus And The Robot
  Arthur Koestler

PRIZES

NOBEL

Literature:

SAINT-JOHN PERSE
FRANCE

PULITZER

Fiction: ALAN DRURY
Advise And Consent

Poetry:
W.D. SNODGRASS
Heart's Needle

History:
MARGARET LEECH
In The Days Of McKinley

National Reporting:
VANCE TRIMBLE
Scripps-Howard

Local Reporting:
JACK NELSON
Atlanta Constitution and
MIRIAM OTTENBERG
Washington Evening Star

International Reporting:
A.M. ROSENTHAL
New York Times

Meritorious Public Service:
Los Angeles Times

Biography or Autobiography:
SAMUEL ELIOT MORISON
John Paul Jones

1960

Love And The French
Nina Epton

The Magician Of Lublin
Isaac Bashevis Singer

Marriage: East And West
David & Vera Mace

May This House Be Safe From Tigers
Alexander King

Memories And Commentaries
Igor Stravinsky & Robert Craft

Miguel Street
V.S. Naipaul

Moments Preserved
Irving Penn

Mr. Citizen
Harry S. Truman

My Life
Marc Chagall

My Adventures As An Illustrator
Norman Rockwell

On Art And Artists
Aldous Huxley

The Other One
Colette

Ourselves To Know
John O'Hara

The Pattern Of Perfection
Nancy Hale

Perle: My Story
Perle Mesta

The Politics Of Upheaval
Arthur Schlesinger, Jr.

Rabbit, Run
John Updike

The Richest American: J. Paul Getty
Ralph Hewins

The Rise And Fall Of The Third Reich
William L. Shirer

Ritual In The Dark
Colin Wilson

The Self-Conscious Society
Eric Larrabee

Sermons And
Soda-Water
John O'Hara

Set This House On Fire
William Styron

Some Angry Angel
Richard Condon

The Sot-Weed Factor
John Barth

The Spirit's Pilgrimage
Mirabehn

Spring Song, And Other Stories
Joyce Cary

The Strategy Of Peace
Senator John F. Kennedy

This Is It
Alan B. Watts

The Tight White Collar
Grace Metalious

Timothy Dexter Revisited
John P. Marquand

To Kill A Mockingbird
Harper Lee

To Sir With Love
E.R. Braithwaite

Trustee From The Toolroom
Nevil Shute

Two Weeks In Another Town
Irwin Shaw

The Violent Bear It Away
Flannery O'Connor

The Waste Makers
Vance Packard

Water Of Life
Henry Morton Robinson

Where The Boys Are
Glendon Swarthout

The World Of Zen
Nancy Wilson Ross

Harry S. Truman

Author of *Native Son* and the autobiographical novel *Black Boy*, expatriate **Richard Wright** dies from a heart attack at age 52 in Paris.

•

Former French Resistance member **Albert Camus**, 46 — writer, philosopher and Nobel Prize winner — dies after his car hits a tree, in France.

•

Doctor Zhivago author **Boris Pasternak**, who won but refused the Nobel Prize for Literature, succumbs to cancer in Russia at age 70.

•

Richard Simon, *the* Simon in Simon & Schuster, dies at age 61 of a heart attack.

•

Editor of the *Dick and Jane* books that continue to teach children around the country how to read, **William S. Gray** dies at age 75.

1960 *Books*

A handwritten version of **E.M. Forster's** *"A Passage To India"* sells for $18,200 in London, setting a record for a living writer's manuscript. In New York, a first edition of **Walt Whitman's** *"Leaves Of Grass"* sells for $3,700.

AMERICAN ACADEMY OF ARTS AND LETTERS

GOLD MEDAL
E.B. White
ROSENTHAL AWARD
John Updike

The British courts decide the unexpurgated version of **D.H. Lawrence's** *"Lady Chatterley's Lover"* is not obscene, and the book goes on sale throughout the country for the first time.

After Miami high schools ban *"1984"* and *"Brave New World"* for being indecent, curious readers buy every available copy in the area. Many community members disapprove of the restriction, which begins when a mother complains about the word erotic appearing in *"Brave New World."*

- **Ken Kesey** is given a grant to complete a novel.

- **Aldous Huxley** becomes a visiting professor at MIT.

- **John Cheever** wins a Guggenheim Fellowship.

- **Saul Bellow** is awarded a **Friend of Literature Award** for "Henderson, The Rain King."

- The **National Book Award** for fiction goes to **Philip Roth** for **"Goodbye, Columbus."**

- In favor of a proposed National Academy of Culture, **Robert Frost** goes to Washington to let some senators know his opinion.

WHAT A YEAR IT WAS!

1960

DISASTERS

In **Chile**, earthquakes and volcanic explosions kill roughly 10,000 people, leave two million homeless and cause 1/2 billion dollars in damage. Tsunamis caused by the massive quakes cause destruction and death as far away as **Hawaii, Japan** and the **Philippines**.

Fires sweep through mental hospitals, killing 225 in **Guatemala City, Guatemala** and eleven in **Kurume, Japan**.

In **Glasgow, Scotland** a whiskey storehouse is the scene of a fire and blast that takes the lives of twenty firemen.

A plane crash in **Copenhagen, Denmark** kills eight members of Denmark's Olympic soccer team.

Two earthquakes in **Agadir, Morocco,** followed by fires and a tidal wave, demolish the city, leaving 12,000 dead and 45,000 homeless.

In **Italy** fifty people perish in flash floods over several days.

In **Vienna, Austria** eighteen people die in a two-streetcar accident.

On the **Amazon River** in **Brazil,** a boat sinks and thirty-two people drown.

A wedding party ends in tragedy in **Lahore, Pakistan** when a house caves in and kills the bride and groom along with other wedding guests.

Devastating heat in **India** and **Pakistan** takes the lives of over 400 people.

Close to sixty Hindus on their way to a religious event drown in the Krishna River in **India**.

Forty children die on **Mindanao Island, Philippines** when a landslide hits their school.

Off the coast of **Senegal** a plane crashes into the ocean, killing all sixty-three on board.

In **South Africa** 417 men die when a coal mine collapses.

1960

During the 4th of July holiday weekend, 442 people die in automobile wrecks nationwide.

Fourteen die and dozens are injured in Bakersfield, California when an oil rig hits a train.

Approximately 40,000 citizens lose their lives on American highways.

Two passenger jets collide over New York in the nation's worst-ever air disaster. One plane crashes in Brooklyn, the other on Staten Island and all the passengers, plus five bystanders, die.

In Toledo, Ohio sixteen members of the Cal Poly football team perish along with six others in an airplane crash.

A bomb is the probable cause of an explosion that destroys an airplane over Bolivia, North Carolina killing all thirty-four on board.

Forty-nine die in a Brooklyn Navy shipyard when an aircraft carrier catches fire.

Eleven Navy men die when two Navy ships collide in foggy conditions near Newport Beach, California.

Hurricane Donna, the worst hurricane to ever hit the Caribbean and the Eastern United States, causes $1 billion in damage and leaves nearly 150 dead. In Puerto Rico, over 100 die.

Painted Hair

There's no limit to what a gal will do to keep up with or a little ahead of the latest fashion.

The latest from Paris – painted hairdos to match mademoiselle's ensemble.

Here we see the artist-hairdresser at work with an assortment of designs.

The question is what happens when she changes her clothes?

Designer Yves St. Laurent agrees with his fellow couturiers of Paris that the big sleeve is passé.

Spring Collection from

Included in the collection is this dress with a gathered skirt which when removed reveals toreador pants (*above left and right*).

Waists are higher, skirts are fuller and the colors gayer than in many a year.

MRS. NIKITA KHRUSHCHEV IS A SPECIAL GUEST AT A VIENNA FASHION SHOW.

he House of Dior

1960 Damsel In A Dress

Waists are usually dropped, hitting the hips, but can also be found Empire style, just under the bust, and occasionally right at the waistline nature gave you. Boat, scoop, square and cowl are your best neckline choices.

Some designers show dresses cut on the bias, popular a few decades ago.

M'lady has many lovely glittery styles to choose from for a night out. For a trip to the theatre, perhaps a Brocatelle suit or a sequined top over a floor length bubble skirt.

Sleeveless is the chic look for dresses and blouses all year long.

Party outfits sure to be a hit include an Edwardian inspired velvet gown or a beaded jacket over a long v-backed silk chiffon dress with a mesh or satin purse.

An enormous bow in front or back adds the final festive touch.

142

1960

WHAT A YEAR IT WAS!

Oleg Cassini is chosen by First Lady-To-Be Jackie Kennedy to produce her new wardrobe. Givenchy and Balanciaga creations currently hang in Mrs. Kennedy's closet.

Oleg Cassini creates formal dresses for female symphony & orchestra members.

Yves St. Laurent is drafted into the French Army for over two years, but is discharged after several months. The House of Dior names Marc Bohan his temporary replacement.

Brigitte Bardot endorses bras for the Atlanta-based Lovable Brasserie Company.

Givenchy releases his first perfumes – *L'Interdit* and *Le De.*

PASSING

Shoemaker to the rich and famous, SALVATORE FERRAGAMO, 62, dies in Italy from a heart attack.

Designer Mainbocher receives the Navy's Meritorious Public Service Citation for designing the WAVES' uniforms nearly two decades ago.

143

1960

THE MAD HATTERS

Spring is in the air as trend-setting designers unveil their hat collections at New York's Waldorf Astoria Hotel. Colors are bright and cheerful, offering a glimpse of a sunnier season just around the corner.

Emphasis is on top-of-the-head with the pillbox especially favored (*far left*) along with the fez (*right*).

HATS OFF TO YOU

Many hats are small, and some cover part of the face. Favorites include the beanie, cloche, cocarde, fez, helmet, pillbox, sailor and turban. Decorations include tulle, sequins, bows and veils.

WHAT A YEAR IT WAS!

145

1960

Pants

continue to grow in popularity, and are the rage in L.A. at Pants Internationale, where designers display form-fitting and loose slacks for any event, day or night.

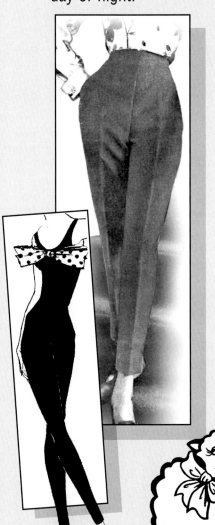

bikini

Despite its ability to turn heads, the bikini is only purchased by approximately 5 percent of bathing suit wearers.

"I" Country
Fashion Contributions

India . . . . *madras, silk*
Italy . . . . *wool knits*
Ireland . . *linen*

FASHIONABLE
BEATNIKS
— or beatnik wannabes —
wear Yves St. Laurent's bubble skirts with slim body hugging tops, in black, of course.

Writer Joan Didion is a Feature Associate with **"Vogue"** magazine.

MISS WOOL OF AMERICA
Patti Jo Shaw

SUIT NEWS

WHAT A YEAR IT WAS!

...other suitable touches

1960

Culottes are seen in suits for the first time, looking like skirts when madame is standing. Previously, culottes were reserved for sportswear. Norman Norell offers his culottes design to any interested designer for free, to insure the pants are made correctly.

An Eton collar or collarless.

Hip-hitting jacket varieties include single or double breasted; button-less or massive buttons; dropped or rounded shoulders; bell or boxy shape; cuffed, short or raglan sleeves.

Skirts are an inch or so below the knees, pleated, tapered, slim, shirred or dirndl style.

Blouses are long and can be the same color as the suit.

Another suit idea is a dress, topped by a long jacket, eliminating the need for a coat.

A FASHION
ISRAEL

Harry Belafonte (left), back recently from a tour of Israel, kicks off the evening's proceedings which features Sylvia Sidney as the commentator. (bottom left)

Both Israeli and American designers combine their talents to produce this distinctive group of fash

WHAT A YEAR IT WAS!

SHOW FOR BONDS

This stunning theatre dress is called "Habima," which is the name of the national theatre in Israel.

Shown here is a beautiful summer evening dress in a cotton print based on an old Yemenite design.

Design skills of two continents are blended for an exhibition that not only delights the eye, but serves a worthy cause as well.

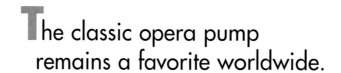

1960

On A Shoe-String

The classic opera pump remains a favorite worldwide.

a lovely evening shoe from the House of Dior is made of satin with bows and spatula toes.

S tockings are colorful with a variety of patterns.

i talian shoes have narrow heels with geometric shapes at the bottom.

Dr. Scholl's Exercise Sandals become available.

150

Bibbidy Baubly You

*L*arge & long & sparkly are the important words. Necklaces are colorful, made of rhinestones, silk or glass beads, crystals, fake pearls or faux stones. Add a tassel for an exotic flair. Multi-strand necklaces reach to the waist or are chunky around the neck, and can be a foot wide.

Bracelets also have several strands.

*B*ig crystal, rhinestone or hoop earrings combined with a large rhinestone flower pin on your suit or hat complete the ensemble, or can even be worn without a matching necklace.

Treat yourself to a head-to-toe designer day of fashion.

Christian Dior
cloche hat

Nina Ricci
damask coat

Capezio
shoes

Pierre Cardin
wool tweed suit

Elsa Schiaparelli
stockings

Maidenform
bra & girdle

Oleg Cassini
bathing suit

LYCRA
foundation garments are introduced.

1960 the Mane Event

Short hair with small curls on the forehead and cheeks is popular with all ages, as are bangs and layers.

The **beehive** is in vogue in London.

The **bouffant** and **bumper coif** are favorite bobs.

Hair should look natural – even if it takes hours of preparation.

For its vacationing clients, **Elizabeth Arden** offers a "coiffure passport," which lists detailed directions and pictures of a hairstyle that any **Elizabeth Arden** beautician worldwide can re-create.

KLM Airlines forbids long hair and gives stewardesses several options of short, fashionable hairdos.

Bows, pins and barrettes help keep hair off the face.

facial facts

COLOR is key in your make-up. Eye shadows are bright, shimmering and can match your outfit. Hues include gold, green, blue, silver, brown and lilac. Lipsticks go beyond the traditional pink and red hues and now include green, blue, yellow, magenta and beige.

Heavily made up eyes are the hottest look in make-up, inspired by a Kees Van Dongen painting from the 1920's.

GOLD DUST on the eyes, cheeks and shoulders and gold flecked lipstick make you look angelic.

The Tonatrone

is a small machine that uses electrical currents to tone your face. The machine exercises the muscles and increases circulation, making sagging chins a thing of the past.

COLORS

Blue, violet, brown, crimson, orange, ruby, purple, beige, plum, yellow, pink, mauve, green.

PATTERNS

Plaid, thick stripes, tweed, paisley, checks, gingham, herringbone, polka dots.

MATERIALS

Chenille, worsted, hopsacking, satin, organza, matelasse, brocade, linen, mohair, velvet, silk, crepe, peau de soie, taffeta, wool knit, chiffon, damask, cotton.

1960

THE WORLD'S BEST DRESSED LADIES

Jackie Kennedy (USA)
Queen Sirikit (Thailand)
Princess Alexandra (Britain)

PERENNIAL FASHION ICONS

Princess Grace, **Merle Oberon** and the **Duchess of Kent** are entered into the exclusive Fashion Hall of Fame.

MERLE OBERON

BEST DRESSED ACTRESSES

Joan Crawford

Marlene Dietrich

Rita Hayworth

Audrey Hepburn

Deborah Kerr

Rosalind Russell

Barbara Stanwyck

Elizabeth Taylor

Lana Turner

BARBARA STANWYCK

AUDREY HEPBURN

Wash and Wear "DECTON," Photographed for Arrow in London

Wherever you go you look better in an Arrow Decton shirt...

The fabulous Arrow DECTON shirt ... of "*Sanforized*" wash and wear fabric that's smooth, luxurious ... and so comfortable 52 weeks out of 52. And what durability! DECTON *outlasts any all-cotton shirt*, because it combines 65% DuPont polyester fiber and 35% long-staple cotton. In white, colors, stripes; favorite collar styles. From 5.00. All-silk tie, 2.50.

ARROW

TRADE●MARK

A FEW FACTS ABOUT 1960

Men's Fashions

80 percent of men's shirts are bought by their spouses.

Pierre Cardin
begins designing menswear.

tie one on

Men purchase 40 percent of ties, with their wives buying the remaining 60 percent. Sir Winston Churchill prefers polka dots on his ties.

Undergarment maker Warner's buys men's shirtmaker Hathaway.

Even if there's no weather report available, the well-dressed man will always know the temperature with his new cuff links and tie clasp that come with a built-in thermometer.

BLACK *is* **men's favorite color for** *shoes.*

new shaving invention

NEEDS NOTHING BUT WHISKERS!

No wires...No water... No sockets...No soap

Why be wired to a wall or shackled to a sink? Now you can shave free as a breeze and feel just as clean. How? Use the New Remington Lektronic Shaver. It gives you the convenience of *cordless* shaving. It gives you razor-close shaves with roller comb comfort.

You can shave anywhere in the world . . . whenever you want . . . actually do other things while you shave. You can read a book, watch TV, avoid the morning bathroom rush . . . do just about anything you want to. You're cleaned up without being tied down. No messy soap suds either.

Try the new Remington Lektronic Shaver soon. It's ideal for trips as well as regular everyday use.

It's the one shaver with everything—needs nothing but whiskers! Yours!

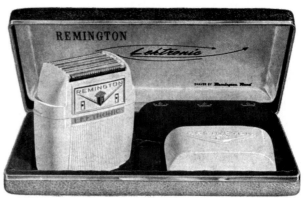

Shave anywhere in the world with the Remington Lektronic Shaver. Any alternating current voltage from 90 to 250 will recharge it. The Lektronic also features Remington's exclusive roller combs that adjust to every beard and skin . . . plus a man-size head, six rows deep.

Product of Remington Rand Electric Shaver Division of Sperry Rand Corporation, Bridgeport 2, Conn.

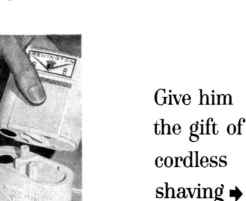

Stores power for up to 3 weeks of shaves. And there are no batteries to replace!

Give him the gift of cordless shaving ➡

New Remington Lektronic Shaver
<small>TRADEMARK</small>

156

SPORTS 1960

A Real Life Cinderella Story

*f*ans gather to watch the Pittsburgh Pirates go up against the Yankees in the World Series.

Yogi Berra is up at bat in the final game *(near right)* and blasts a 3-run homer *(far right)* to put New York in the lead 6-4 in the 6th inning.

Then a double-play ball hits Yankee Tony Kubek in the throat putting two men on base.

*L*ast time the Pirates played in a series was in 1927 and the Yanks won four straight.

The lead seesaws until the bottom of the 10th when Pittsburgh's Bill Mazeroski slams a 4-bagger *(right)* to end the game and the series with victory for the Pirates *(bottom)*.

WHAT A YEAR IT WAS!

1960

BASEBALL ● NEWS

New York Yankees manager since 1949, Casey Stengel is given a mandatory retirement at 70 after racking up ten American League Pennants and seven World Series Championships. Ralph Houk chosen successor.

World Series

PITTSBURGH PIRATES
over
NEW YORK YANKEES
4-3

Home Run Leaders

National League
Ernie Banks (Chicago, 41)

American League
Mickey Mantle (New York, 40)

RBI Leaders

National League
Hank Aaron (Milwaukee, 126)

American League
Roger Maris (New York, 112)

Batting Champions

National League
Dick Groat (Pittsburgh, .325)

American League
Pete Runnels (Boston, .320)

Most Valuable Player

National League
Dick Groat (Pittsburgh)

American League
Roger Maris (New York)

Rookie Of The Year

National League
Frank Howard (Los Angeles)

American League
Ron Hansen (Baltimore)

THE PAY CHECKS:

Gil Hodges	$39,000
Duke Snider	39,000
Wally Moon	30,000
Don Drysdale	27,000
Carl Farillo	25,000
Charlie Neal	24,000
Clem Labine	23,000
Roger Craig	17,000
Sandy Koufax	17,000
John Roseboro	16,000
Larry Sherry	14,000

39-year old Stan Musial of the St. Louis Cardinals is asked to take a pay cut from $100,000 to $80,000 and agrees the cut is overdue.

NATIONAL LEAGUE PITCHERS DON CARDWELL OF THE CHICAGO CUBS AND WARREN SPAHN AND LEW BURDETTE OF THE MILWAUKEE BRAVES EACH PITCH NO-HIT, NO-RUN GAMES DURING 1960 SEASON.

THE NEGRO AMERICAN LEAGUE BECOMES THE LAST SEGREGATED BASEBALL ASSOCIATION TO DISBAND.

NEW YORK APPROVES PLANS FOR SHEA STADIUM TO BE LOCATED IN FLUSHING.

NATIONAL BASEBALL LEAGUE VOTES TO GRANT FRANCHISES TO NEW YORK AND HOUSTON EFFECTIVE IN 1962.

AMERICAN BASEBALL LEAGUE GRANTS PERMISSION TO MOVE THE WASHINGTON, D.C. FRANCHISE TO MINNEAPOLIS–ST. PAUL, AND TO INITIATE A NEW CLUB IN WASHINGTON AND A FRANCHISE IN LOS ANGELES. THE NEW LOS ANGELES FRANCHISE TO BE HEADED BY COWBOY MOVIE STAR GENE AUTRY.

CONSTRUCTION OF DODGER STADIUM BEGINS IN LOS ANGELES AFTER CONCLUSION OF CHAVEZ RAVINE CONTRACT LITIGATION.

Going Out On A High!

September 28th: Today is the last day Boston Red Sox star Ted Williams will be up at bat and he says goodbye to his sparkling career by hitting a 420-foot home run against the Baltimore Orioles making it his 521st career homer, the third highest in baseball history.

CY YOUNG AWARD
VERNON LAW
PITTSBURGH PIRATES

WHAT A YEAR IT WAS!

1960 ADVERTISEMENTS

Enjoy Sports Again

A. Ravielli

Research finds new fast way to shrink hemorrhoids without surgery

Today there's a fast new way to shrink hemorrhoid tissues, stop pain and itching—all without surgery. The name of this medication: The PAZO Formula.

CLINICALLY TESTED BY DOCTORS. The PAZO Formula does *more* than just shrink hemorrhoid tissue. It also contains specific ingredients to relieve pain and itching promptly, fight infection, promote healing, and lubricate membranes.

WORKS FAST. Soon after using The PAZO Formula, you sit, stand, walk, and enjoy active sports in *comfort*. This superior over-all medication brings symptomatic relief even to long-time pile sufferers.

AVAILABLE NOW in stainless suppositories or ointment at your druggist's. Get faster, more complete relief without surgery. Get ...

The PAZO® Formula

Another Fine Product of Grove Laboratories

IN SKIING...

EXPERIENCE

IS THE GREAT TEACHER

IN SCOTCH...

TEACHER'S

IS THE GREAT EXPERIENCE

Othmar Schneider, Olympic Ski Champion, instructor and ski film producer.

Only experience could produce Scotch of such unvarying quality and good taste as Teacher's Highland Cream.
Today, the fourth and fifth generations of the Teacher family still personally supervise the making of this famous product of Wm. Teacher & Sons. Ltd.

BOTTLED IN SCOTLAND

TEACHER'S HIGHLAND CREAM BLENDED SCOTCH WHISKY / 86 PROOF
SCHIEFFELIN & CO., NEW YORK, N. Y.

159

1960 NATIONAL LEAGUE

67,000 fans gather in Philadelphia to watch the hometown Eagles play against Green Bay for the NFL Crown.

The Eagles' Van Brocklin (*far* passes to Tommy McDonald (*center right*) to wipe out an early Green Bay lead for a score of

Bart Starr (*below*) fires to Max McGee (*above*) for a score and Green Bay leads again.

As the last quarter opens the Packers charge back with Tom Moore doing the running on this play.

WHAT A YEAR IT WAS!

FOOTBALL 1960 CHAMPIONSHIP

The Eagles trail 13-10 when their rookie back Ted Dean runs back to kick off 58 yards to the Green Bay 40.

Dean takes the handoff, (right) rounds the end on a wide sweep for a touchdown (bottom) and Philadelphia beats Green Bay 17-13 for its third World Football Championship.

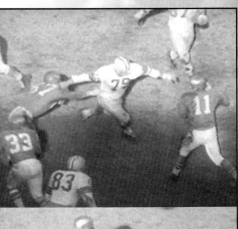

Two plays later Van Brocklin *(top)* passes to Billy Barnes *(bottom)* and they're on the 13.

1960 HEISMAN TROPHY

Joe Bellino Joins The Immortals Of College Football

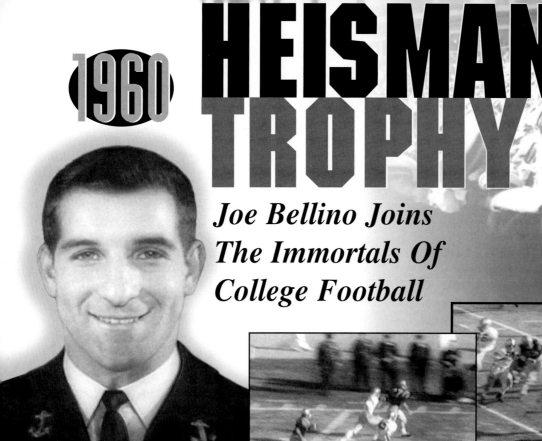

Navy star halfback Joe Bellino is this year's winner of the Heisman Memorial Trophy as well as winner of Philadelphia's Maxwell Trophy making him twice honored as Outstanding College Football Player of 1960. One of the highlights of his outstanding record is that he's the only Navy man to score three touchdowns in one game against Army.

This 58-yard run from Navy's one turned the tide against Army in the first quarter.

A few plays later Bellino scores the first touchdown against Army.

The fans go wild.

Army's desperation effort is a long pass for the score that would have won (*above*) and saves the game for Navy (*right*).

Famous Births 1960

Marcus Allen

Roger Craig

John Elway

Ivan Lendl

Greg Louganis

Cal Ripkin, Jr.

Fernando Valenzuela

FOOTBALL

NATIONAL FOOTBALL LEAGUE CHAMPIONS

Philadelphia Eagles over Green Bay Packers 17-13

AMERICAN FOOTBALL LEAGUE CHAMPIONS

Houston Oilers over Los Angeles Chargers 24-16

COLLEGE FOOTBALL COACH OF THE YEAR

Murray Warmath
Minnesota

NFL RUSHING LEADER

Jim Brown
Cleveland
1,257 yards

Rose Bowl

WASHINGTON over WISCONSIN 44-8

NATIONAL COLLEGE FOOTBALL CHAMPIONS

Minnesota

The first American Football League games begin in the United States with the Eastern Division consisting of Boston, Buffalo, Houston and New York and the Western Division including Dallas, Denver, Los Angeles and Oakland.

1960 — BASKETBALL

NBA CHAMPIONS
Boston over St. Louis **4-3**

NBA ASSISTS
BOB COUSY, Boston **715**

WILT "THE STILT" STATS

NBA SCORING LEADER
WILT CHAMBERLAIN, Philadelphia 2,707 points

NBA MOST VALUABLE PLAYER
WILT CHAMBERLAIN, Philadelphia

NBA ROOKIE OF THE YEAR
WILT CHAMBERLAIN, Philadelphia

Chamberlain takes the game by storm breaking all scoring records as a 1959-60 rookie with the Philadelphia Warriors becoming the first NBA Rookie of the Year.

On hearing about Wilt Chamberlain's new rock 'n' roll recording, Dolph Schayes of the Syracuse Nationals exclaims: *"I hope he sells a million copies. Then maybe he'll quit basketball."*

NCAA CHAMPIONS
Ohio State *over* California **75-55**

COLLEGE PLAYER OF THE YEAR (DIVISION I)
OSCAR ROBERTSON

CELTICS crush KNICKS for record 59th win this season.

WHAT A YEAR IT WAS!

NBA 1960 CHAMPIONSHIP

14,000 people jam the Boston Garden for the final game of the hard-fought NBA championship.

Boston Celtics (white) meet the St. Louis Hawks in the final and deciding game.

Bob Cousy with the ball plays one of his greatest games in a brilliant career.

The final score is 122-103 and Bob Cousy is the man of the hour!

The Hawks stay with the Celtics right through the first quarter then the Celtics move ahead. Right down to the final tick of the clock the Celtics dominate the play.

1960

FigureSkating

U.S. Champions
Dave Jenkins
and **Carol Heiss***

World Champions
Alain Giletti, FRANCE
Carol Heiss, U.S.

*Carol wins fifth straight world figure skating title in Vancouver, B.C.

HOCKEY

STANLEY CUP CHAMPIONS

Montreal Canadiens over **Toronto Maple Leafs** 4-0 winning their fifth consecutive championship.

CALDER MEMORIAL TROPHY (ROOKIE OF THE YEAR)

BILL HAY, Chicago

ROSS TROPHY (LEADING SCORER)

BOBBY HULL, Chicago

LADY BYNG MEMORIAL TROPHY (MOST GENTLEMANLY PLAYER)

DON McKENNEY, Boston

HART MEMORIAL TROPHY (MVP)

GORDIE HOWE, Detroit

VEZINA TROPHY (OUTSTANDING GOALIE)

JACQUES PLANTE, Montreal

A right winger with the Montreal Canadiens for his 18-year career and first player in National Hockey League history to score 50 goals in 50 games, Maurice "The Rocket" Richard retires from the game.

WHAT A YEAR IT WAS!

CAMEL RACING:

[first organized camel racing season in Jordan is held at the Royal Club track in Amman.]

Winner: Al-Yatima
ridden by Ouden Sleiman (Bedouin)

POWDER PUFF DERBY

Pilot: **Mrs. Aileen Saunders,**
El Cajon, California

Co-Pilot: **June Douglas,**
Fall River, Massachusetts

[Flew a Cessna 172 at 145 m.p.h. from Torrance, California to Wilmington, Delaware – a distance of 2,509.13 miles.]

TOUR de FRANCE
GASTONE NENCINI
ITALY

1960
horse racing

KENTUCKY DERBY
VENETIAN WAY,
ridden by
W. Hartack

BELMONT STAKES
CELTIC ASH,
ridden by
W. Hartack

PREAKNESS
BALLY ACHE,
ridden by
R. Ussery

HORSE OF THE YEAR
KELSO

AP ATHLETE OF THE YEAR

MALE (Track)
Rafer Johnson

FEMALE (Track)
Wilma Rudolph

CAR RACING

INDIANAPOLIS 500*

Jim Rathmann
Ken-Paul Special (138.8 mph)

Just prior to the race, a temporary scaffold collapses killing two spectators and injuring around 75.

WORLD GRAND PRIX*

Jack Brabham, Australia

Grand Prix racing comes to California for the first time, the race taking place in Riverside. This is only the second such race in the U.S.

LE MANS

Oliver Gendebien and Paul Frare

INDYCAR

A.J. Foyt

WHAT A YEAR IT WAS!

SUMMER

ROME, ITALY

The First Summer Games Covered By U.S. Television

The games attract a record 5,348 athletes from 83 countries.

The Winners:

BOXING
U.S. Boxing Team wins three golds with Cassius Clay, 18-year old boxer from Louisville, Kentucky, winning the Olympic Light Heavyweight Crown beating Polish opponent Zbigniew Pietryskowsky. Clay doesn't take off his Gold Medal for two days.

DECATHLON:
UCLA teammates **Rafer Johnson** and **C.K. Yang** finish 1-2 in the decathlon. Johnson breaks decathlon record.

BASKETBALL:
An easy U.S. win is basketball with the greatest amateur basketball team ever assembled including **Oscar Robertson, Jerry West, Jerry Lucas, Walt Bellamy** and **Terry Dischinger.**

DIVING & SWIMMING:
Diver Gary Tobian wins first U.S. Gold and swimmer Chris von Saltza wins three Gold Medals for the U.S.

GYMNASTS:
Russia's Boris Shakhlin and Larissa Latynina.

TRACK & FIELD:
- The U.S. wins 9 track and field titles including repeat medals for Lee Calhoun, Glenn Davis and Al Oerter.

- Sprinter Wilma Rudolph is first woman to win three Gold Medals for the U.S.

- Australia's Herb Elliott runs 1,500 meters in 3 minutes, 35.6 seconds.

- Jumper John Thomas, who set a new Indoor Jump world record at the Millrose Games held at New York's Madison Square Garden by jumping 7 feet, 1-1/2 inches, sets another high jump mark of 7 feet, 3-3/4 inches during Olympic trials.

Barefoot marathon runner Ethiopian Abebe Bikila wins a Gold Medal breaking the record by almost 15 minutes.

- America's Ralph Boston wins the Gold breaking Jesse Owens' Olympic Broad Jump Record, flying 26 feet 7-3/4 inches into the air.

OLYMPIC GAMES

WHAT A YEAR IT WAS!

WINTER — 1960
SQUAW VALLEY, CALIFORNIA

HOCKEY:

U.S. wins its first Olympic hockey championship beating Canada and the U.S.S.R. Canada takes second place.

Skiing

Canada's Ann Heggtveit wins the first Gold Medal for her country.

Figure Skating
WORLD CHAMPS

MEN
DAVE JENKINS (U.S.)

WOMEN
CAROL HEISS (U.S.)

SKATING PAIRS:

BARBARA WAGNER

and

ROBERT PAUL

Canada

Who Got The Gold?**

U.S.S.R.	7
GERMANY	4
UNITED STATES	3
NORWAY	3
SWEDEN	3

**When one winner's gold medal begins to peel, it is discovered that the gold medals are not really gold but gold-plated.

PROFESSIONAL GOLFERS' ASSOCIATION

H JAY **EBERT**

PGA
PLAYER OF THE YEAR
Arnold Palmer

MASTERS
Arnold Palmer

BRITISH OPEN
Kel Nagle

U.S. OPEN
MEN: Arnold Palmer
WOMEN: Betsy Rawls*

* Sets record by becoming the first golfer to win the Women's Open Championship four times.

LADIES PROFESSIONAL GOLFERS' ASSOCIATION

W MICKEY **RIGHT**

PGA/LPGA
LEADING MONEY WINNER
Arnold Palmer, $75,263
Louise Suggs, $16,892

U.S. AMATEUR / U.S. WOMEN'S AMATEUR

Deane Beman
JoAnne Gunderson

No More Sunday Blues

Pennsylvania's Blue Law banning golf on Sundays is repealed along with ban on picnics, tennis, boating, swimming, bowling and all other healthful or recreational activities.

CHESS

WORLD CHESS CHAMPION	U.S. CHAMPION

MIKHAIL TAL, U.S.S.R.

BOBBY FISCHER (16-Years Old)

JAMES E. SULLIVAN MEMORIAL TROPHY

Rafer Johnson, *TRACK*

DOG SHOW

Westminster Kennel Club
Chick T'Sun
of Caversham

Pekingese

U.S. OPEN

MEN:
NEALE A. FRASER
over
ROD LAVER

WOMEN:
DARLENE HARD
over
MARIA BUENO

Wimbledon

MEN:
NEALE A. FRASER
over
ROD LAVER

WOMEN:
MARIA BUENO
over
SANDRA REYNOLDS

Davis Cup

AUSTRALIA
over
ITALY
4-1

ARTHUR ASHE,
17-year old senior honor student from St. Louis and sixth-seeded in tournament, out-seeds Frank Fruehling in 4-hour match to become first Negro winner of National Junior Indoor Tennis Title.

BOWLING

AMERICAN BOWLING CONGRESS TOURNAMENT
SINGLES:
PAUL KULBAGA Cleveland, Ohio (726 Pins)
ALL EVENTS:
VINCE LUCCI Trenton, N.J.

National Bowling League Is Formed.

WOMEN'S INTERNATIONAL BOWLING CONGRESS

SINGLES: **Marge McDaniels,** *Mountain View, N.J.*

ALL EVENTS: **Judy Roberts,** *Angola, N.Y.*

Bowling Proprietor's Association of America – U.S. Open

HARRY SMITH   **SYLVIA WENE***

*First woman to roll more than one sanctioned 300 game when she scores a perfect game in both the World Invitation Tournament and the National All-Star.

ABC MASTERS

BILLY GOLEMBIEWSKI
Detroit (874 Pins)

MRS. MARION LADEWIG
Grand Rapids

*C*assius Clay (*white trunks*)
challenges eastern heavyweight champ
Gary Harrish who is in trouble from
the first round on.

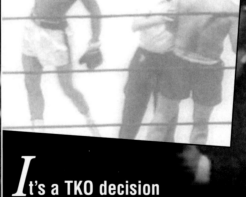

*I*t's a TKO decision
for Clay and more points for
the Windy City team which wins 12 out of 16 bouts.

B O X I N G

1960

HEAVYWEIGHT
Floyd Patterson
knocks out Ingemar Johansson in the 5th round becoming first boxer to regain heavyweight title.

OLYMPIC LIGHT HEAVYWEIGHT CHAMP
Cassius Clay

WELTERWEIGHT
Benny "Kid" Paret

FEATHERWEIGHT
Davey Moore

LIGHTWEIGHT
Joe Brown

LIGHT HEAVYWEIGHT
Archie Moore

MIDDLEWEIGHTS
Gene Fullmer
Paul Pender

Swede Ingemar Johansson is first foreigner to be chosen S. Rae Hickok Pro Athlete of the Year.

Louisville, Kentucky's
CASSIUS CLAY
Settles In California And Turns Pro.

The 20-Month Old National Boxing Enterprises Is Dissolved.

Paul Pender takes middleweight title from **Sugar Ray Robinson.**

SUGAR RAY

1960 WAS A GREAT YEAR, BUT...

THE BEST IS YET TO COME!